Called

By

The

Protector

By

Ronna M. Bacon

ISBN 978-1-998821-25-9

Exodus 14:14. The Lord will fight for you, and you have only to be silent.

Deuteronomy 316. Be strong and of good courage, do not fear nor be afraid of them; for the Lord your God, He *is* the One who goes with you. He will not leave you nor forsake you.

NKJV

Table of Contents

Chapter 1

Standing in the doorway to her arts and crafts gift shop, Finnlea Galbraith stared in horror at the destruction that faced her. The front door had been broken in and was in pieces, and the security system destroyed. She stepped through, watching for the debris on the floor. Horror continued to build inside her as she read the spray-painted warning on the walls. *You will pay. We will be back. You have something that we want. You will give it to us or pay the price.*

Finnlea almost ran from the building, her phone in her hand. She stared at it, not quite sure who to call or even why to call. She was new to the town of Grenview, just moving there in the spring. Her hands shook with fear, shaking enough that she wasn't able to find the numbers to make a call. Finnlea stared around at the small plaza, not seeing anyone who had done this. Yet, she felt watched. Moving here? She thought that she had finally left the past behind her. Only it didn't seem to be that way.

A voice speaking beside her had her jumping and screaming. Her long auburn waves moved with her motion, fascinating the man who had approached her. Her hazel eyes were huge with fright as she stared at him.

"I'm sorry?" Liem Steele wasn't quite sure what had happened. He waited for the lady to speak. When she didn't, he moved to look through the door. *This is not good. Someone did a number on her shop.*

He turned back to face her, finding her staring at him, fright on her face.

"Are you okay?" His deep blue eyes held his concern for her. "What happened?" The sun reflected off the red-gold hair that he had cropped a little longer than was the normal hair cut for men in these days.

"What happened?" Finnlea's voice rose in pitch as she spoke. "You just looked in there. What do you think happened?" Her words had a bite to them, a bite which was not normal for her.

"I can see that it's trashed. But why? Who did you anger? And who's after you?" Liem's hand was out to draw her away from the store. "Have you called anyone yet?"

"Called anyone? Who would I call?" Finnlea's thinking was not clear, not one bit.

"The police, for one. And your landlord, for another." Liem waited somewhat impatiently for her to speak. He had simply stopped in the plaza to grab breakfast from his favourite coffee shop. To find a lady in distress had not been in his plans, but it looked more and more as if it had been in God's plans for his day. He had spied her just standing outside her shop and curiosity had drawn him that way.

"I'm sorry. I didn't mean to take your time." Finnlea waved her hand at him. "Go on. I'll be just fine." She wrapped her arms around herself, fear rising even higher inside her. Whoever it was that had tracked her before in her hometown seemed to have followed her to her new town. Finnlea was not ready for that and not sure who she could turn to or even trust.

—

8

Liem walked away and stopped a few feet from Finnlea, his eyes on her as he assessed her. His phone was out as he called to report the break-in to the police detachment, knowing that a patrol officer would respond and quickly. It was how their town worked.

"Listen. I was only here to grab some breakfast. Can I get you something?" Liem waited patiently for her to speak, a sigh rising within him when she refused to respond. *Okay, Lord. She needs my help, I guess. I just don't know what I can do other than to stand by her and wait with her. I mean, my skills as a carpenter are not what is needed, not right yet. And I fear for this lady. She's in danger and trouble and needs someone to stand beside her and stand in the gap between her and her enemies. Does it really have to be me?*

Finnlea looked around as she heard tires on the pavement. She frowned, feeling as if that had been her totality of emotions that day. She stared at the men who exited the vehicle and ran towards her. She screamed and turned, her feet moving her as quickly as they could towards where Liem had headed. It was not enough. She was tackled and taken to the pavement, the pavement scraping at her exposed flesh. Hauled roughly to her feet, Finnlea was pulled towards the vehicle, fighting to escape even as that happened.

Liem turned back from where he had walked away, shock on his face. His own feet picked up their pace as he raced towards Finnlea and tackled the man holding her. The three tumbled to the ground, Finnlea screaming as she hit the pavement once more.

Liem in turn was tackled by one of the other men who held him to the ground with a knee on his lower back. His own wrists now bound in front of him, Liem was dragged to his feet and shoved roughly forward. He could hear Finnlea protesting at their treatment before a savage blow stopped her words. He struggled once more to free himself. Ladies were not treated like that, not in his presence. A blow to his back sent him to his knees, winding him and driving his vision to darken.

Shoved into the vehicle, the couple shared a look. Liem was angry, angrier than he had ever been in his life, he decided. Finnlea was terrified. She struggled to escape and to free her hands, reaching for the door handle before she was dragged away from it. A gag covered her mouth, stopping the angry words that she was spouting at the men. Finnlea glared at them, anger sparking from her eyes.

Liem mentally shook his head. He had no idea who these men were but shouting at them was not helping. He had no idea why they were abducted and abducted they were. They were strangers to one another. All he had done was stop to try and help a lady in distress.

***

The patrol officers walked through the building, puzzled looks on their faces. It was not like Liem to call something in such as this and then disappear. One of the officers ran for the coffee shop, a sudden thought in his mind. The video feed showed what he had feared. The couple had indeed been kidnapped.

Chapter 2

Finnlea struggled to escape from the hands that pulled her from the vehicle, spinning to face the man. She had managed to pull the gag down from her mouth during the drive. She was not happy, not at all, and angry that the events of the day had just been taken from her hands.

"Let me go!" Finnlea spit the words at the man, her eyes narrowed and angry. "Let me go back to my shop. I don't have anything that you might want. In fact, I don't even know you."

The man gave a cruel laugh and then just shoved her towards the barn that they had parked near. Finnlea dug in her heels, not prepared to do what they said. The man just wrapped his arms around her abdomen and picked her up. Finnlea screamed and struggled to escape, her feet kicking at the man and her hands shoving at his arms. He groaned as her heel struck his shin.

Liem, pulled from the other side of the vehicle, shook his head, frustrated once more. He wanted to tell Finnlea to stop fighting the men. Yet, he had to admire her spunk. She was not taking being abducted quietly, as much as he would have preferred that for her. Liem was shoved roughly forward, stumbling on the rough ground.

The barn was well built and solid. Liem studied it as best as he could. There just didn't seem to be a way out of it, not that he could see with a cursory glance. He could hear Finnlea still fighting with the man before he turned to face them.

Finnlea was dropped to the ground, landing on her hands and knees. She scrambled up and ran to Liem, knowing somehow that he would do his utmost to protect her. She just didn't know how she could tell that, but she could. Reaching him, she stood slightly behind him, knowing that he would do what he could to protect her.

Liem watched the men, his head turning to watch as two of them walked around them. He wasn't sure what was happening or why they had been abducted. *Lord, I don't know why or who, but You do. Protect us, Lord. Help me to find a way to get Finnlea out of here and to safety.*

The tallest and oldest of the men walked back to stand in front of them. A sneer covered his face. Liem was not to be there. He could work with that, he decided. His hand reached out to grasp Finnlea's hair, tugging her forward. Finnlea gave a small scream again, her bond hands up in an attempt to pull herself free. It didn't work. The man simply pulled her harder towards the other side of the barn.

With her hair freed, Finnlea spun to stare at him. A frown covered her face. He looked familiar, but she wasn't sure where she knew him from. Her eyes lit on Liem, finding him just standing there and watching her. She could tell that he wanted to help her but the revolver held to his side prevented that.

"You have what we want. You will provide it to us. Maybe then you two will live." The man's rough and coarse voice broke through the silence. "And you will provide it now."

"I have what you want? I have no idea what you are talking about." Finnlea stepped backwards from him forward motion until she hit the barn wall and could move no further backward.

"You have what we want. You will provide it. You have two hours to tell us where it is." The man moved closer to her, a threat in his bearing, before he turned and walked away.

The couple heard a lock click shut with a loud snap. Finnlea leaned back against the wall, fear rising within her. She had no idea what the man wanted. She just knew that she didn't have anything that belonged to anyone else.

Liem walked towards her, his hands reaching to untie her bonds. She did the same to him, her eyes on his face. She frowned, not sure what to think of this man standing in front of her. She wasn't used to a man stepping in like he had.

"You okay?" Liem kept his voice low, uncertain if they were truly alone in the barn.

Finnlea nodded, a hand resting on her cheek.

"I think so. But what about you?"

Liem shrugged, knowing that he had taken harder blows playing sports.

"I'm okay. I've been hit worse than this. Now, about what they wanted? Do you have it?" He stared at her as she snorted before he gave a grin. "I take it that's a "no"."

"It is. I have no idea what they want. And before you ask me, I don't know them. At least, I don't think that I do." Finnlea was puzzled at being taken hostage or whatever it was that someone would call it.

Liem stared at her once more before he gave a low laugh. Finnlea was not impressed with that. Before she could even open her mouth, Liem's hand went up.

"I didn't think that you did. Now, let's see if we can find a way out of here." Liem walked away, searching for a way out and not finding one. His head turned as he heard a noise and stood in the middle of the barn, a frown covering his face. Finnlea was on her way up a ladder, heading for the haymow. He sighed, his head dropping forward for a moment before he simply followed her.

Chapter 3

Liem watched as Finnlea climbed the ladder before he walked across the barn floor. His scuffed steel-toed work boots kicked up debris, dirt, and dust from the floor. He stood, hands on the ladder, watching as she confidently climbed upwards.

"Finnlea? Get back down here! You don't want the men to catch you up there." Liem waited almost impatiently for her to respond. When she didn't, he shook his head and reached for the ladder as well, climbing up after her.

Finnlea stood for a moment in the haymow before she began to search. Liem watched her, not sure what she was up to. He sighed. This was not how his day was to go. He had been due on a jobsite and now he wasn't there. Liem's eyes narrowed as he thought through what had happened. He shook his head as he couldn't figure it all out. No, he decided, he didn't know the men. He certainly didn't know what they had asked Finnlea for. He wasn't sure if she did either.

Turning in a circle, Finnlea searched the haymow, finally seeing what she wanted. She headed for the door or window or whatever it was called. Liem's hand went out to grasp her arm, stopping her in her tracks. She stopped, anger on her face for a moment.

"Finnlea? Stop! We need to make a plan." Liem frowned at her, his voice stern and almost harsh in his fear for her.

"Why?" She broke free from him and continued to walk towards the opening.

Liem followed her, reaching out once more to stop her. He felt her tense under his hand and he dropped it from her arm.

"Finnlea?" The question is his voice stopped her for a moment. "Just what are you looking for?"

Finnlea stared at him, shocked that he had no idea what to find. She shook her head at him and walked away once more. Liem could not believe his eyes that she had done it again. He was becoming more and more worried about her. He could see that she was afraid but determined not to show it to anyone. Just how he would help her, Liem was not sure. He just knew that he was not walking away from her then or in the near future.

"Just what are you searching for?" Liem finally stood beside her, watching with a slightly amused look on his face despite the danger that he could tell that they were still in.

"A hay elevator. We could lower it and climb down." Finnlea rubbed at her cheek, leaving a dark streak of dust on it. "Or the rope that is usually tied at the hay door." Spotting something in the hay, she pounced on it, holding up the end of a rope. "This! This is what I'm looking for!"

Liem had to grin for a moment at the triumphant look on her face before he sobered. His eyes traced the rope to where it was knotted on the top beam of the hay door. He leaned through the door to stare at the ground and then searched for cover. He felt

Finnlea beside him and watched in disbelief as she threw the rope out of the door and then shinnied down it. Liem sighed to himself and followed. He just had to. Finnlea was going to get herself hurt or worse, killed, or else end up back in captivity.

Liem's hand stopped her in her tracks once more, this time his grasp tight enough so that she could not escape it. He searched for cover and then tugged her with him towards a building nearby.

"Let me go!" Finnlea hissed at him in a low voice. "I am quite capable of going that way. It's where I was heading anyway."

"Finnlea! Stop! We need to get undercover." Liem glanced down at the watch on his right wrist. "It's almost two hours since they left. Do you not realize that they'll come looking for us? We need to find somewhere to hide."

"I know that." Finnlea pointed to their left. "That way. The corn is high enough that you won't be seen. How tall are you anyway?"

Liem groaned. She just wasn't letting it go in her determination to be independent. He reached for her hand and pulled her with him towards the field. Disappearing into it, he dragged her with him at a rapid pace. Liem glanced down at her feet and was thankful that she had sensible shoes on and not the high heels that a lot of ladies wore.

"Liem? Stop, please!" Finnlea pulled him to a stop. "I need to rest for a moment. And you didn't answer my question."

"What? The one that asked how tall I am? I'm over six feet. That doesn't matter. What matters is why you were abducted." Liem watched her closely, concern for her on his face.

"I don't know." Finnlea spun as a loud yell was heard from behind them. "They're in the barn. They'll find us." Finnlea was away from Liam, running as fast as she could.

Liem followed her, his long legs covering the ground rapidly. He reached for her hand, tugging her through the corn and then across a road and into a forest. He was afraid for her and he really didn't understand why. Liem just begged God to protect the lady with him.

Chapter 4

Their steps slowed as fatigue hit them and hit them hard. Liem searched for somewhere to rest, tugging Finnlea with him towards a towering maple tree. He shoved her down on the ground and sat himself, back to the tree. His head went back against the rough bark of the trunk as his eyes closed. Liem needed a break and a breather. His forearms rested across his upraised knees.

The songs and chirps and calls of nature sounded in his ears. He didn't hear anything that sounded remotely human. He prayed fervently that they had escaped. They just needed to determine where they were and call for help.

Finnlea dropped her head to her knees, her arms wrapped around her legs. She couldn't take another step. And she decided that she was very thirsty without anything that she could drink to alleviate that. Her head turned for a moment, a hand raised to rest on her cheek that hurt from the blow she had taken earlier. A frown fluttered across her face as she studied the man with her. He had come to her rescue without any thought about harm to himself. Finnlea didn't know any man who would have done that in her hometown. Hope began to raise in her that perhaps she had finally found a town to belong to. The church family had been friendly and reached out to welcome her.

"Liem?" Finnlea's voice was low and almost inaudible. "Are we safe?"

Liem's head rolled against the tree trunk. He studied the lady with him, seeing her fear but also her determination to survive and succeed. The ice packed tight around his heart started to melt bit by bit. He had blocked out any hope and plan of a romance. Now, this beautiful and spunky lady had dropped right into his life. Liem knew that they would part ways once this adventure or whatever it was called was over. He didn't want that.

"For now, I think we are. We can rest for a bit." Liem reached for her hand, gripping hers in a loose way before his head was down and he was praying for her. When he looked up, he didn't turn back to her. He kept his eyes on the area around them. "God is with us, Finnlea. He is here. He is our protector and defender in all things. Sometimes? Sometimes He allows things and events into our lives. It could be to teach us something or it could be to bring someone to justice. I have had friends who have gone through this. A friend has a saying that summarizes it all. He states that God has a plan and purpose for us that we may not understand here on earth."

"Your friend is wise." Finnlea bit at her lip, not sure how to continue to ask what she needed to. "Liem? Do you know where we are?"

"In a vague way. I recognized the farm. I just didn't expect to be taken there." Liem reached for his phone, staring at it for a moment before he swiped across the face of it to wake it up. "I have service. Let me call someone to come and get us."

"They would do that? Even out here. We're miles from town, aren't we?" Finnlea stared around her, afraid for the moment. She wasn't used to being out in the forest and felt very much out of place there.

"They will. I'll call my brother. He's a private investigator and will come and find us. By now, I suspect that he has already been told that I'm missing and that you likely are as well. We're tight that way." Liem's voice died away for a moment. Sadness wafted across his face, causing Finnlea to frown at him for a moment. His finger went up as he called his brother. "Lorcan?

"Liem? Where are you? And are you okay?" Lorcan ran for his truck, knowing that he had to find his brother. Liem would simply tell him where he was.

"I am, for now. And so is Finnlea. Hers is the store that was damaged today. You were there?" Liem was confident that his brother had been. Lorcan had a sense of when danger was hitting at someone he knew and just appeared to be there for them.

"I was. Paul called me when he identified your truck. Now, where are you?" Liem drove away from his home.

"In the Banks woods. We're near the stream. Finnlea and I managed to escape our abductors. I'll need to find Paul."

"He's looking for you as are the patrol officers. We didn't know that you had been taken out of town." Lorcan turned his truck that way. "I'll be about twenty minutes. Can you stay out of trouble for that long?" He grinned as Liem laughed.

"We'll try. Just be careful, Lorcan. They want something from Finnlea. She has no idea what." Liem pocketed his phone, knowing that he needed to charge it soon.

"Liem?" Finnlea waited for Liem to turn towards her. "Your brother? He's coming to find us?"

"He is, Finnlea. He is. Come on. Up on your feet. We'll head that way and find the road. He'll find us in about fifteen minutes. The problem will be staying out of sight of the men who abducted us. They'll be watching all the roads around here."

"That is a problem, isn't it? And if we end up back in their hands, we won't get away again, now will we?"

Liem agreed silently, his hand reaching to pull Finnlea to her feet. Surprising her, he wrapped her into a hug and then with her hand in his once more, headed towards the road. He knew the men would be looking for them. And he didn't want Finnlea to fall back into their hands. Liem was afraid that Finnlea would simply disappear and he didn't want that. A lady had come into his life. This lady was one who he wanted to get to know better.

Finnlea walked beside Liem, quiet for the moment. She studied him, seeing his strength of character but also the worry that he was trying to hide. *Lord, You did this, didn't You? You brought Liem into my life at a time when I needed someone. I didn't know that I did, but You did. He's someone I think would make a great friend. Only, we're in danger and I don't know that we'll be safe.*

Chapter 5

Waiting somewhat impatiently for Lorcan to arrive, Liem stood in the shadows of the trees. He had tucked Finnlea away behind a large oak tree despite her protests. He had grinned to himself, admiring her spunk and feistiness. He just worried that it would get her into deeper trouble. The sound of a vehicle approaching them and then slowing to a stop sounded in his ears. Liem waited, knowing that if it was Lorcan, he would find his brother.

Lorcan stopped his truck near the woods, his eyes searching for his brother. Liem had to be here somewhere, he decided. He climbed down from his truck, heading for the woods on the other side. He had left the doors unlocked. Liem would simply tuck himself and the lady with him away in the back seat. He heard the truck door close quietly and then walked back to climb in. Lorcan's eyes were on the move, searching for anyone who might be watching for them. He saw no one.

Liem had waited for Lorcan to head for the other side of the road before he tugged Finnlea with him and tucked her into the truck. She protested every step of the way, albeit in a low voice, asking how he knew that this truck was safe. He had simply told her to hush and that this was his brother's truck. Liem told her that he thought he could trust his own brother.

Driving away, Lorcan glanced at the back seat, seeing Liem with his head up just enough so that he could watch out of the window. His glance caught the female form struggling to rise from the floor but held there by Liem's hand. Lorcan grinned to himself. Liem, he decided, had found his lady and she was fighting him all the way. Serves him right, he muttered to himself.

"Lorcan, did you see anyone?" Liem's voice was low even though it didn't need to be.

"No, I didn't. I was careful. It took a little longer than I thought. I drove by the farm. There's a lot of activity there. They're searching for you two. I would love to know how you escaped from them." Lorcan kept his eyes on the road, glancing once in a while at his brother.

"By the rope tied to the hay door. How else would we escape?" Finnlea's voice held a snap to it.

"I see. And just how did you know to do that?" Lorcan's voice held laughter which he was trying hard to stifle. He could see the look of disbelief on Liem's face.

"That's what I would like to know." Liem moved his hand and let Finnlea sit on the seat. He pointed to her seatbelt. She snapped it closed around her, a dark look on her face that said she was going to do that anyway. He didn't need to be so bossy.

"From my Gramps. He had a farm and allowed the grandkids to play in the haymow. We weren't supposed to use the rope but we always did. He would tell us off but one day, he just came up as we were using it and did the same as us. It was a wonderful day." Finnlea sniffed as she remembered that day.

"That sounds like a wonderful memory, Finnlea." Liem watched her closely before he looked up and caught his brother's eye. He shook his head. He had no idea what was going on and he didn't know that Finnlea would know either.

"Finnlea? Where do you want to go?" Lorcan spoke at last, his voice breaking through her memories.

"My store. I need to see what is there." Finnlea stared out of the side window, not seeing the compassionate glances sent her way.

"We can do that, but I can tell you one thing for sure. They will not let you into it. Not yet. They are still working through their investigations." Lorcan sent a look of sympathy towards Finnlea, seeing how she was fighting back her emotions. "We'll stop and you can speak with the investigators. And Liem, you both need to give your statements before you say much more of anything to anyone."

"We know that. Who was there?" Liem knew most of the investigators on the force.

Lorcan slowed as he entered the town and drove carefully towards the plaza where Finnlea had her shop. He was not certain that she should be there or how safe that she would be, but she needed to go there. Where she went after that, he was not sure. Lorcan just knew that she was still in danger and because Liem would not leave her, he was in danger. He sighed to himself. And that meant that he was in danger as well.

Finnlea watched as Lorcan pulled into the plaza and parked as close to her store as he could get. Police tape still surrounded the scene with an officer obviously visible in a cruiser parked right in front of the door. She was shocked to see that it was still a crime scene. She was sure that she could just walk in and take stock of what had happened.

"Lorcan, is Paul around? And can we get permission to let Finnlea walk through her store?" Liem's hand was warm and strong on Finnlea's as he grasped hers.

"He would be. He said to call him late this afternoon. He'll need your statements, you know." Lorcan shut off the motor and then shifted to watch the pair in the backseat.

"He does. Call him and let him know we're here." Liem's head went back on the seat as his eyes closed. He was praying for his new lady friend, knowing that she faced something drastic in the next few weeks. He would not walk away from her. His eyes opened to study the fading sun. It was getting late and he was exhausted. Liem turned to Finnlea, finding her staring out of the front window of the truck, a shuttered look on her face.

Lorcan was out of the truck, pacing, with his phone to his ear. Paul had been surprised when Lorcan simply stated that he had Liem and Finnlea with him. He was on his way, he said. Could Lorcan please keep them out of trouble? Lorcan had laughed at that.

Liem shoved open the door as he saw Paul approaching him. He sighed. They would need to give their statements before they entered Finnlea's store.

That was not something that he was looking forward to.

Finnlea was out of the truck and almost running around to slide to a stop in front of Paul. Hope was on her face that she could finally see her store. She prayed that it was not as bad as she had thought.

Paul studied her before he simply shook his head. He didn't think that he had ever had a victim run towards him as she had.

"You're the detective? I can go into my store?" Finnlea barely drew in a breath as she waited for his agreement to that.

"I am. I'm Paul Wright. Let me get your statements and then we'll walk through your store. I'm sorry about it. It's not in great shape." His face grimaced with sympathy as hers crumpled for a moment.

Finnlea had had an idea that was what he would say. She stiffened her backbone as her father would have said and prepared for the worse.

"Then, who do I talk to and do just that?" Finnlea's words almost tripped over one another as she gave Paul her statement. She also tore the papers from his hands before she scanned them and then signed her statement.

Liem's face was a picture of disbelief and then resignation as he watched Finnlea. Paul had another detective come by and take his statement. He leaned against Lorcan's truck as he waited for Finnlea to finish. Lorcan stood shoulder to shoulder with his brother, an amused look on his face. *She's just the one he needs, Lord, isn't she? He needs someone feisty and spunky and who stands up to him. He likes to take charge. She won't let him. But I still worry, dear Lord, about them. Please protect them.*

Chapter 6

Two hours later, Finnlea paced the parking lot, watching her store. It was obvious that she would not be able to access her store that day. Liem walked into her path and stopped her, surprising her by wrapping his arms around her.

"Tomorrow's Sunday. We'll come back around and see if they have released it. Lorcan is willing to help. Our friends will help as well." His chin rested on the top of her head.

"I need my car and it's behind that tape." Finnlea was angry. She had been kidnapped, threatened, and now faced losing her business. She didn't know that Lorcan had already reached out to the artisans that he knew, simply asking for help. Word was spreading rapidly among that community and her store would be restocked in no time.

"I can't get to my truck but Lorcan will drop you off, and we'll pick you up in the morning." Liem stared down at the lady he still held. "We'll grab breakfast, hit the early service, and then come this way."

Finnlea pushed away from him, anger still sparking from her. She glared at Lorcan who stood by his truck, his gaze flickering between his brother and his lady. He had the time to wait, patience in situations something that he had learned.

The next morning, Finnlea glared at Liem as he stood beside Lorcan's truck. He grinned at her as she did that.

"In you go, Finnlea." Liem was well aware that Lorcan had chosen the classic that the brothers had lovingly restored and that it had a bench seat. That meant Finnlea would need to sit between the brothers.

Finnlea heaved a sigh and climbed into the truck. Lorcan grinned at her before he drove away, heading for a local diner. The church service that followed their meal was exactly what they needed, Liem decided. God was their Protector. They needed to trust Him to do that.

The police tape was gone by the time that Lorcan parked near the store. The brothers exchanged a compassionate glance before Liem wrapped an arm around Finnlea. The men's prayers filled the cab of the truck but did little to ease Finnlea's stress.

Finnlea shoved at Liem, forcing him from the truck. She stalked towards her store, taking in the boarded up window and then headed for the front door, her keys out to open it. Liem gently took them from her and unlocked the door. He shoved it open, not sure what they would find. Paul had given him a head's up the night before.

Finnlea entered her store, dismay and a sense of loss filling her being. She looked around, devastated at what she saw. It had taken her months to get her store to where it had been. She just didn't know if she could start over. He has won once more, she decided. Finnlea blinked back tears, feeling Liem's arm around her and heard his whispered prayer for her.

Liem and Lorcan walked through the store, pausing at last. They looked around before walking over to where Finnlea stood.

"Finnlea?" Lorcan's voice had her looking up at him. "I reached out to some artisan friends. Some of them are your sources. They are reaching out to other friends." He was surprised as Finnlea hit out at him, not seeing the smirk on Liem's face. "Finnlea?"

"Don't ever go behind my back. Thank you though." Finnlea stared at the store, her mind muddled as to what she could do. She turned as she heard Liem's voice.

"We will work with you, Finnlea. Lorcan has started an investigation all ready. Talk to us. What do you want to change or improve in here. Write them out and we will make them happen."

Finnlea glared at him. Who was he to make plans for her?

Liem continued to grin at her. She was right, he knew.

"Make your plans, Finnlea. Put down your dreams and wishes. We'll make them come true. Our Bible study group will be here tomorrow to help clean up. Another friend will drop off a dumpster for the garbage. They don't want to repaid. They want to be the hands and feet of God."

Finnlea nodded grudgingly. She was used to doing things herself. There was resentment welling inside of her that she had to rely on others. There just was no other option.

Rising from her desk late that night, Finnlea stretched and walk through her house. She no longer felt safe there. She just didn't know why. Finnlea smiled as she thought about Liem. He was beginning to take over her thoughts.

Liem rose from his knees in the early morning hours. He had spent time in prayer after spending hours on plans for the store. He paused in his walk towards a shower and clean clothes. Finnlea was taking over his thoughts as well. She was feisty and not afraid to stand up for herself.

Morning light found Finnlea unlocking her store's front door. She nodded at the men who were to replace the windows that had been shattered. She walked through the store, knowing that her dreams were shattered.

Liem watched her, sorrow for her on his face. He walked towards her, his footsteps sounding loud in the silence. Finnlea spun, fear on her face. Liem dropped the paperwork on the counter and swept her into a hug,

"Okay, sweetheart?" Liem didn't realize that he had called her that.

"I don't know." Finnlea shoved away from him. "This is a lot of work. Maybe I should just walk away from it."

"Don't do that. I worked on some plans that you can use or not."

"You do?" Finnlea walked away, her attention on getting to work on salvaging what she could.

Lorcan stopped beside his brother, an amused look on his face. He shook his head. Liem had it bad, he decided. And he would help this romance along.

Chapter 7

Late that afternoon, Finnlea stood behind the new counter that held a new cash register. Liem stood beside her, an arm around her. She didn't seem to notice that as her gaze roamed her store. To say that she was surprised and grateful would be an understatement. The store looked brand-new. The group that had descended on her store that morning had sorted through the debris, rescuing what they could. New flooring had been laid. The walls were coated with fresh paint. New shelving units were beginning to hold new items for sale. Finnlea had a hard time controlling her emotions. She had not expected to be ready to open once more in the morning. She still did not understand how it had all been accomplished. The store now looked like her dream store.

Lorcan paced around the store. He knew that the security system had been upgraded but he still planned on working there for the next few days. He grinned as he imagined the look on Finnlea's face when he told her that. Liem would be on his jobsite instead of where he wanted to be.

Liem walked away from Finnlea, heading outside. It had been a long day but a good day. He dropped a kiss on her cheek before he did walk away. Lorcan caught the look of surprise on her face and bit back a smile. He waited to see how she would react.

Finnlea's hand hit her cheek before she was almost running after Liem. The back door swung shut behind her as she hit the parking lot and then circled

---

the building looking for Liem. He was standing near his truck which he had parked near the back of the building

"What was that all about?" Finnlea stomped towards him, the sound of her voice turning him to face her. She was glaring at him.

"What was what?" Liem was puzzled. He had no idea what she was talking about.

"This!" Finnlea's finger poked at her face. "What you did!"

Liem was still puzzled.

"What did I do?"

"You kissed my cheek! Liem! What were you thinking?" Finnlea's voice was almost a wail.

"I did, didn't I?" Liem reached to wrap her in a hug, simply holding onto her as she struggled to escape his hug. "I'm sorry. I should not have done that."

"Liem! Make up your mind. Either you meant it or you didn't!"

"I did mean it, Finnlea. You looked as if you needed a hug. And a kiss." Liem grinned down at her.

" Liem! Did we just go somewhere with our friendship? We don't know each other well enough for this to go any further." Finnlea turned and walked away, Liem's arms dropping back to his sides.

Liem watched as she did just that. He turned himself and walked towards the store, seeing Lorcan waiting for him. Finnlea had disappeared into the store.

Liem's head dropped as he thought through his actions. This was not him to do that or to approach a young lady in that manner.

Lorcan watched Finnlea as she stomped inside. He was not able to read her and that was very unusual for him His eyes turned to his brother. Something was happening that affected Liem. He feared for his brother and the lady who was now entwined in Liem's life.

"Liem? Are you okay?"

Lorcan's voice reached through Liem's muddled thoughts. He looked at his brother and then past him at the closed door.

"I'm not sure, Lorcan. I really am not." He sighed, knowing what Lorcan was asking. "I am interested in Finnlea. I worry about her, though." Liem scrubbed at his face. "How do we keep her safe?" He knew what he was asking of his brother.

"Let's find your lady and get her home. I'm planning on working here for the next few days." Lorcan grinned. "I'm not sure how Finnlea will take that." He jumped as he heard a voice behind him.

"You're what? Since when?" Finnlea stood behind Lorcan, hands on her hips.

Liem struggled to control his laughter. He walked away, heading around the building to the front of it. His steps slowed before he sighed. A hand reached for his phone as he studied the message spray painted on the store wall.

Paul walked towards Liem, a frown on his face. His thoughts were dark before he began to pray for his friends. Lorcan stood beside Finnlea who now had Liem's arm wrapped around her.

"Liem? You didn't see anything?" Paul stared at the warning that clearly threatened Finnlea.

"Not a thing. And the cameras have been spray painted as well. That's frustrating as we just put them up. Lorcan checked the feed. All we can see is a gloved hand." Liem was angry and knew that he had to turn that over to God. He just wasn't ready to.

Finnlea had finally stopped shuddering in fear and was too growing angry. God was there. She could feel His presence and heard His call to her to come to Him and let Him protect her.

Paul walked towards the crime scene tech, engaging that lady in conversation. Both of them were frustrated, to say the least. They just didn't have enough information to move forward with the case. Paul and his team had found the property where the couple had been held. There had been no evidence there that could be found. The owners, who were out of town on vacation, had been shocked when Paul had contacted them. They had been unable to provide any information about who may have had access to their property.

Chapter 8

The next morning, Finnlea unlocked her store door and walked into it, reaching to turn off the security system. She could hear Lorcan right behind her. His hand went out to stop her before he walked through the store, searching for anything that was out of the ordinary. He found nothing.

Finnlea frowned as she moved through the store, readying it for the day. A reporter for the local newspaper was due in mid-morning. Finnlea was not sure that she was making the right move with the interview but she was determined to showcase her clients rather than herself.

Liem had listened to her the night before as they shared a meal at a local diner. He knew Finnlea well enough to know that she would have prayed through her decision. Liem had prayed for her, his hands reaching for hers. All he could do was alert Lorcan to be ready for anything.

Lorcan stood in the office doorway two hours later, watching as Finnlea moved through the store with the reporter. He nodded. Finnlea was being very careful, redirecting the reporter away from what had happened to her and to the store itself. Liem would be happy to hear that.

Finnlea walked towards Lorcan, grateful for the mug of tea that he was holding out to her. She had emphasized that she would not tolerate any reporting about the crime that she was involved in and would take legal steps if necessary. If the reporter was willing to write a story on her store, that was acceptable. The reporter had been startled at that. Her purpose had been a story on the crime but had agreed to frame the story as a followup to another reporter's article and how the store was reaching out to local artisans.

"Okay, Finnlea?" Lorcan studied her face, knowing that Liem would want to know how she was.

Finnlea shrugged. She was not sure how to feel. She had felt her phone vibrating in her pocket during the interview. It had been difficult to ignore. She had been praying that Liem would reach out to her.

"I am not sure, Lorcan. How am I supposed to feel?" She moved past him, her mug of tea hitting her desk. Finnlea sighed. This was not her to feel so discouraged and afraid. She was not sleeping well and didn't know how to overcome that.

Lorcan watched her for a moment before he pulled out his phone. It was Liem, he noted, as he moved away to take his call.

"Liem?"

"Lorcan? How is she?" Liem was almost holding his breath as he waited for Lorcan to answer.

"She's hurting and not sleeping. The interview went as we expected. The reporter kept trying to bring up what had happened. Finnlea threatened legal action. I think that Paul needs to reach out and stop the reporter from doing that."

Liem agreed. He had had just such a talk with Paul that morning. Paul had not been happy about the interview. He had reached out to the publisher after he hung up from Liem. The publisher had not known about the interview but agreed that he would ensure that no details of the crimes went public.

"How did the interview go?"

"I'm not sure. Finnlea is quiet. You'll need to ask her that."

Finnlea sighed to herself. She wanted to see Liem but she was afraid to. She was afraid that she was bringing danger to him.

Liem stood at Finnlea's house door later that afternoon. He grinned as he heard the muttering approaching the door and braced himself. Instead, as Finnlea opened the door, he simply wrapped her into a hug. Finnlea surprised them both by hugging him back. He walked her into the house and shut the door behind them. Liem's keen eyes studied her.

"Okay, sweetheart?"

Finnlea shrugged. She was not sure if she was. Not any more. Finnlea shot a glance towards the kitchen. Her mail was scattered on the floor, dropped there when she saw that plain white envelope.

Liem's face grew grim as he stalked that way. He stared down at the mail before he was calling Paul.

An hour later, Paul approached the couple. Liem had tucked Finnlea into his truck as they had waited for word on what the letter said. Lorcan stood shoulder to shoulder with his brother. He had finally convinced Finnlea to let him start an investigation into what was happening.

"Paul?" Liem's voice brought Paul's head up as he stopped walking.

"Liem?" Paul looked past Liem towards Finnlea. That lady was staring back at him, her face shuttered. He could see the worry and fear that she was trying hard to hide.

"What did the letter say?" Finnlea's voice was low.

Paul sighed. She went right to the heart of the matter.

"It was a threat, Finnlea. A direct threat that you will die. Do you know who is doing this?" Paul's voice was stern.

"No, I don't. I'd be in their face if I did know." Finnlea scowled at him. "Isn't that what you would do?" She could see the brothers' shoulders shaking at her words. A slim forefinger poked Liem in his shoulder.

"I would but then again, I'm trained to do that. We need to talk again and that will be tomorrow."

Finnlea was not happy with that. She needed to be in her store. And she was prepared to fight him on that.

Chapter 9

Saturday found Liem walking through Finnlea's store. He was happy to see the number of people who were there. He searched for her, finding her at the cash register. He wrapped an arm around her which caused her to frown at him.

"Let me run the cash for you." He grinned at her before she nodded and moved away.

Finnlea looked around late that afternoon finding that Lorcan and Paul had both appeared. She frowned at them as well, causing both men to grin at her. Liem walked up to her and swept her into a hug. She glared at him before she hugged him back.

"Ring off your cash, sweetheart. And then we'll find something to eat."

Finnlea stared at him, thinking that he was overstepping but shrugged she moved off to do what he had asked. She scurried to prepare her bank deposit, finding Paul's hand there to take the bag with the deposit and the key needed to make the deposit. Finnlea was being taken care of. She just didn't know how she felt about that.

Seated beside Liem in a booth at a favourite diner, Finnlea listened to the three men as they joked around and found herself drawn into their fun. She shivered at one point and looked around. Someone was watching her. And she didn't know who.

Liem's hand tightened on hrs in a warm clasp. He could feel the eyes watching them. He would not give them the satisfaction of looking around.

Paul rose at last, heading for his home. He was deeply troubled by the danger that surrounded Liem and Finnlea. There was just not enough information to determine who or why.

Liem paced his home that night, thinking through what he knew. Lorcan had handed him a folder and just looked at him without saying a word. Liem had not opened it as yet. He was not sure if he really wanted to. He knew that Lorcan would be fair with what he had found. He sought his rest at last, praying for his lady.

Early the next morning, Liem was out on a local running trail, needing that time by himself and His Lord. He prayed through his usual list, ending with a cry from his heart that God would protect his lady. Absorbed as he was in his prayers, Liem didn't hear the loud roar of the ATV that sped towards him. Roused at last, he shot a look over his shoulder and then try to dodge out of the way. He just didn't make it in time. A glancing blow sent him spinning away from the track and into the brush that lined it. His body rolled over and over before it landed with a thud against a decaying tree trunk. Liem didn't move from where he landed and certainly didn't hear the maniacal laugh that sounded through the air before the ATV sped off. It was early enough in the morning that no one was around to see the attack.

Shifting restlessly on her chair in the church, Finnlea watched for Liem. He had not arrived to pick her up as he had promised. She had then taken her own way to church. She jumped as Lorcan sat beside her.

"Finnlea? You're on your own?" Lorcan was surprised at that.

"I am. Your brother didn't show up or bother to call." She stared back at him. "So, where is he?" She settled back to get through the service, not sure what to think.

Lorcan's phone was out before he was on his feet, stepping out of the sanctuary to try and reach his brother. He was unable to do so. Paul, who was one of the ushers that day, approached him.

"Lorcan?"

Paul's voice drew Lorcan's eyes to him.

"It's Liem. He didn't show up at Finnlea's this morning. And I am getting no answer to a phone call or a text message."

"There isn't?" Paul spun in a circle. "Stay with Finnlea. I'll be in touch." After a quick word to one of the other ushers, Paul almost ran from the church. He walked around Liem's yard, not seeing any sign of him. Liem's truck was missing. That fact worried Paul. Where was his friend?

Lorcan had followed Finnlea to her home, parking behind her car while she locked it and ran to jump into his truck. He waited for her seat belt to click over her before he drove rapidly away. He stopped at Liem's home, finding Paul waiting for him.

"No sign of him?" Lorcan prayed that his brother was there.

"Not a one". Paul leaned against the truck. "Where would he have gone?"

Lorcan's fingers tapped on the steering wheel. His thoughts were troubled. *Where are you, Liem? This is not you. You always answer at least a text message. Lord, protect my brother. I don't know where he is but You do. Lead us to him.*

Finnlea stared through the windshield of the truck. Her thoughts were troubled. Liem had begun to take over her thoughts and prayers. He was stepping in to try and protect her as much as she emphatically denied that she needed one. She watched as Paul walked back towards the patrol officer waiting for him.

"How do we find him?" Finnlea's voice was barely audible as she fought against her emotions.

"Let's head back to your place. You need to change from your good clothes." Lorcan shot a glance at the sky. It was growing more and more overcast. He was afraid that his brother was out there somewhere and injured.

Finnlea drew in a deep breath as she pulled on a sweatshirt over her lightweight sweater. She was afraid for Liem, worried that he was either hurt or worse even than that dead.

Lorcan turned to watch her as she paced her kitchen. His mouth opened and closed without him uttering a word. He had tried to track his brother's phone without success.

A sudden loud crash had Finnlea jumping and uttering a low scream. She stared at Lorcan, terror on her face.

"What was that?"

"Thunder." Lorcan walked quickly to the living room window. He drew in a deep breath. The rain was teeming down with frequent flashes of lightning and crashes of thunder that just seemed to have no starting point or ending point.

Finnlea had allowed him, to stand beside him. This was not what they needed. All she could do was pray for her friend.

Chapter 10

An arm shoving at the ground, Liem shakily sat up with his free arm reacting to wrap around the tree trunk. He swiped at his face, trying to wipe away the rain and unable to do so. He slumped against the fallen tree, too sore to rise but knowing that he could not remain there. His head dropped against his arm as he lost his fight to stay alert.

Footsteps sounded hours later as the rain was beginning to ease. The two men paused, sharing a look. They had found the man that was missing. One of the men drew Liem upright and then draped him over his shoulder. The men retraced their tracks to the parking lot. Liem's keys were pulled from his pocket before the truck door was unlocked. He was unceremoniously dumped on the back seat before the two men jumped into the front seat. The truck sped away, not towards help but towards a farm just inside the town limits. It was parked inside the garage before the door closed behind it.

Pulled from the truck and once more draped over the man's shoulder, Liem was carried to a hidden room in the garage. He was dropped roughly on the bunk there before the two men turned and walked away. They drove away from the farm in Liem's truck, heading for a local wrecking yard. In less than an hour, Liem's truck had disappeared into a chunk of twisted metal. Lim would not be tracked that way.

Liem roused once again in the night, in pain and cold. He reached for a blanket to wrap around himself. A hand was pressed against the side of his head in an effort to ease the pain. He dropped back into darkness, not knowing that both Lorcan and Finnlea were desperate to find him or that Paul was in a desperate search for him as well.

The next morning, Finnlea stood at the start of the running track, not sure if she should be there. She hadn't told anyone where she was heading. Her store was closed as usual on the Monday. She sighed at last and began her walk along the trail. Liem loved this track and was a runner. Finnlea prayed that she would find him. She just didn't think that she would.

Two hours later, Finnlea leaned against her car. She had been correct in her opposition. She had found no sign of him on the trail. She had not left the track or trail or whatever it was called.

Lorcan had tracked her down. With Paul beside him, he too leaned against her car, not saying a word.

"Lorcan?" Finnlea's voice was barely audible."Is he here and in the woods?"

"It is possible. Paul has asked for some officers to respond and help search. Our local search and rescue team is on its way." Lorcan turned to Finnlea, seeing the worry that she was trying hard to hide. He missed her feistiness and began to pray for her and for his missing brother.

Paul stopped an hour later as an officer called his name and then beckoned to him. He moved rapidly that way, not sure if Liem had been found or not.

"What do we have?"

"In there. We think someone was against that fallen tree. Evidence is suggesting that. They're gone now. We just don't know where." The officer looked around, frustrated at not finding Liem. "The dogs aren't able to pick up any scent."

Paul was frustrated as well. He turned to watch Lorcan and Finnlea, seeing as Lorcan seemed to persuade Finnlea to leave with him. Lorcan drove away, following Finnlea. Paul turned back to the investigation that didn't seem to be going anywhere. It was now over twenty-four hours since Liem had disappeared.

Lorcan turned from starting the coffee in his kitchen and then went to find Finnlea. They had walked through Liem's home. Lorcan had noted that Liem's running her was missing. That fit with what they had decided Liem had done.

Finnlea looked up at Lorcan. To say that she was very worried was an understatement. Her feistiness had dimmed for now and that saddened her.

"Lorcan? Is this okay?" Finnlea had been working on a missing person poster.

"It is. I'll email it to the printer and pick it up later. Our friends are meeting here in the morning." He watched her. "What about your store?"

"It's covered. One of the ladies volunteered to work it. She's works retail before." Finnlea was trying her best tasty upbeat, but it wasn't working.

"That's good." Lorcan rose and returned with mugs of coffee for them. "We'll find him, Finnlea."

"I have no doubt that we will I just don't understand why. All he did was come to my aid."

"That may have been all it took. We don't know who that was." Lorcan had been investigating Finnlea and her past, with her consent. He hadn't found anything. It was at the point where he was ready to reach out to fellow investigators. Liem's disappearance had paused that thought. And the newspaper article had just spoken good of her store.

"Where is God?" Finnlea's quiet words broke through the silence. Her hands cupped the mug, finding the heat soothing.

"He is here, Finnlea. He is in the midst of this. He is calling us to come to Him for protection." Lorcan didn't look up.

Finnlea rose and walked through the house, setting her mug on the kitchen counter. She then just kept walking out of the house and towards her own home. She didn't see the patrol vehicle that followed her home.

Lorcan roused from his thoughts an hour later as a knock came at his door. Paul stood there, the bundle of flyers in his hands.

"Paul?" Lorcan was surprised to see him.

"In the house, Lorcan. Did you know that Finnlea walked home? A patrol vehicle followed her home." Paul was angry at the circumstances.

"She did?" Lorcan rubbed at his face. "Somehow that doesn't surprise me. Paul, where does that investigation stand?"

Paul shook his head. The investigation was stalling and he had no idea where to look next.

Chapter 11

Rousing once more, Liem rolled to his side, pulling a blanket around himself. The shivers that had been afflicting him were lessening. That was good, he decided. He just didn't realize that he was running a fever. A hand reached for the water bottle on the stand by the bed before he drank deeply and then set it back on the stand. He looked around the room, not sure where he was but knowing that it was not his home. Liem's eyes closed as he dropped into unconsciousness once more. He had no idea that it had been well over a day since he went missing.

Two days later, Liem sat up shakily on the side of the bed. His head was buried in his hands before he looked around the room. He didn't realize that he was repeating what he had done each day.

Staggering to his feet, Liem felt along the walls, not finding a doorway. His head dropped back as he stared at the ceiling and the skylight in it. His head dropped forward as he squeezed his eyes closed. Unable to stay upright, his body dropped to the floor. His last conscious thought was a prayer to God to free him.

Finnlea paced her store that day, worried about Liem. She had chosen not to be part of the search teams that day. Instead, she had prayed for Liem and Lorcan. Her prayers had included the search teams and the investigative teams.

Lorcan trudged towards his home, fatigued beyond what he had ever experienced. He knew it was because Liem was missing. The searching done that day had not produced any leads. That fact left him feeling devastated and more worried than he had been. Finnlea had called him at noon, just to pray with him.

Her store locked behind her, Finnlea trudged towards her car, looking up as she heard footsteps. Fear momentarily flickered across her face. The patrol officer took her keys to unlock her car before he searched it inside and outside. Finnlea frowned as he did so, taking her keys from him. She had an escort, she knew, and didn't like it. Paul had arranged that for her.

Her Bible caught her attention that evening. She sighed and reached for it. Lorcan had been in touch, just confirming that she was safe at home. Her head bowed over the Book as she searched for comfort, peace, and strength. Setting aside the Bible, she reached for a blanket and wrapped it around herself. Finnlea slept, not hearing the slight noise at her door.

Night passed, the moon sailing through the night sky and the stars that sprinkled the deep blue of the night sky. The remand purple of the breaking dawn soon streaked the eastern sky. Lorcan was on his feet and stretched. He headed for his back deck. He was exhausted but had found some information that he needed to go over with Finnlea. That would need to wait until later. He had work that needed to be done before he reached out to her.

Paul walked the running track that afternoon until he reached the spot where it was thought that Liem had left the track that day. His feet took him towards the tree trunk. He stood and wished that the tree trunk could speak and tell him what had happened. He turned at last, pausing for a moment. Paul shook his head, knowing that the crime scene techs had done their best. The rain had washed away any trace of what had happened there. He was also troubled that there had been no sign of Liem's truck. As far as anyone could determine, Liem had no enemies. The thought was that he had disappeared to terrorize Finnlea.

Finnlea walked her store once more, her thoughts troubled. Her day hadn't started off on a good note when the patrol officer arrived to escort her to work. That lady had not let her out of the house until the investigation and search had been completed. The note taped to her door had threatened her and she had no idea why.

Lorcan looked up from his work, the sound of the doorbell disturbing him. On his feet, he headed for the door. Looking out of the window, he frowned. He could not see anyone out there. He stepped out onto the front porch and searched for whoever it was. A rushing sound caught at Lorcan's attention. He wasn't able to avoid the hard knotted fist that landed on his jaw. He crashed to the front porch floor, unconscious. He didn't feel the letter that was dropped onto his chest. The man walked away, his task completed.

Night had fallen by the time that Lorcan roused. He sat up slowly, a hand to his jaw. He wriggled it. At least it was not broken. He stared at the white envelope that he held. A frown covered his face before he walked slowly back into his home. Searching for his phone, Lorcan hesitated before he called Paul. That call went straight to voice mail. He sighed before he reached for an icepack and headed for the living room where he slumped on the couch. The envelope was dropped on the couch beside him. Lorcan decided that he would open it soon. Instead he slept, his body needing it.

Paul retrieved his voice mail messages, frowning as he heard the pain in Lorcan's voice, squinting at his watch. He would track Lorcan down in the morning as it was now after midnight. At the moment, he needed to sleep.

Lorcan simply handed Paul the letter in the morning. Paul had simply appeared at his door. He had read it not that long before Paul had appeared. It didn't say much other than that Lorcan was being watched. His brother's life depended on his actions. The letter was not clear what they expected of him.

Paul was puzzled as well. There was nothing in the letter to indicate that the writer knew where Liem was or that they had him in their control. That would have been useful information.

"Paul? What do you make of this?" Lorcan's finger flicked at the paper. He had told Paul what had happened the night before. It puzzled both men.

"I really don't know what to think, Lorcan. Whoever it is seems to be watching both you and Finnlea very closely. She thinks that they have been in her store, posing as customers. We can't be with both of you all the time."

"No, you can't. She's too independent to let anyone smother her. She's going to be out there searching."

"And we can't stop her. Not that she would let us." Paul was frustrated and sleep deprived. He was due for a week off and didn't want to take it. He was being given no choice in the matter.

"I know, Paul. She needs Liem. He is reaching her whereas we can't." Lorcan rubbed at his jaw, knowing that a bruise had formed.

"You're not going to be able to hide that from Finnlea." Paul grinned as Lorcan scowled at him.

Lorcan sighed. What Paul had just said was only too true. Finnlea would dig until she had all the details that he wasn't ready to share with her.

Chapter 12

Lorcan strode towards Finnlea's store, a bag of food in his hands. He was worried about his brother's lady that day. He lifted up the bag of food to show Finnlea who nodded.

Finnlea moved towards her office, knowing that was where she would find Lorcan. Her steps slowed before she turned to stare back at her store. She missed Liem more than she thought possible. She prayed for him to come home and soon. Then she sighed again. Liem was in God's hands and protected by Him. Liem would come home in God's timing.

Staring at Lorcan, Finnlea slowly sat in the chair behind her desk. She took with thanks the container of food that he was handing her. His prayer filled her with peace.

Lorcan waited for Finnlea to speak, a gleam of mischief in his eyes. Their shared meal finished, Lorcan gathered up the debris as he listened to Finnlea speaking with a customer. The store was getting busy. He watched as Eve, one of the ladies from their Bible study group, walked towards him.

"Lorcan? Any word on Liem?" Eve tucked her purse away. She had been hired to work in the store. Finnlea had realized that she needed help even though she felt very dangerous to know.

Lorcan shook his head. He needed to talk to Finnlea about the letter that he had found. He just had to stop her movements.

———

Finnlea approached Lorcan during a lull mid-afternoon. She sat and watched him. Lorcan looked up from his work, nodding.

"Lorcan? What did you receive? And how did you get that bruise?"

Lorcan nodded before he told her exactly what happened to him the night before. Finnlea's face crumpled in fear for a moment before it hardened. She was determined to find Liem and find him that day.

"Where would they hide him?"

"That I don't know. It's somewhere that he can't escape from. And his truck?" Lorcan had searched for it without any luck.

"It has likely been destroyed by now. Isn't that what they do? Can we ask Paul?"

Lorcan shook his head.

"He's away for the next week." Lorcan was frustrated at that but knew that Paul needed his vacation.

"He needs that break. Go home, Lorcan. I'm closing now." Finnlea watched as Lorcan walked slowly towards his truck.

Standing in her kitchen that evening, Finnlea was torn. She needed to sleep yet something was keeping her up. A small sound at the door had her spinning that way, a hand to her throat. She moved on tiptoes towards the door, stretching to look out of the peephole. Surprise held her still for a moment before she was fumbling to unlock the door and pull it open. The tall man who stood with one hand on the wall stared at her before he reached to wrap her into a hug and moved her into the house. He shut the door behind him before wrapping his lady into a tight hug.

Finnlea was floored. Liem was there and held her in his arms. She was shocked to say the least. Liem's body was swaying before his legs collapsed. His fall took both of them to the carpeted floor where he lay still, his lady still wrapped tight in his arms.

Finnlea was still for a moment, too much in shock to move. Then, she began to struggle to escape Liem's arms. She knelt beside him, rolling Liem to his back. She could not rouse him. Scrambling to her feet, she ran to find her phone.

"Lorcan? I need help." She tossed her phone on the kitchen counter, not hearing Lorcan yelling at her, asking her why. Finnlea reached for a cloth and wrung it out in as warm a water as she could. Back on her knees beside Liem, Finnlea washed at his face, hearing the moans and then the soft sighs that he uttered.

Lorcan slammed his truck door shut behind him and ran for Finnlea's house. He twisted at the door knob, surprised that the door opened under his hand. He stood for a moment, shock on his face before he shoved the door closed and he was on his knees beside his brother

"Finnlea? Where did Liem come from?" Lorcan's hands were assessing his brother.

"He just showed up here. I can't get him to wake back up." Tears were close to the surface and she hated that.

"He just showed up?" Lorcan sat back on his heels before he reached for his phone. Liem needed help that neither Finnlea nor he could give.

Twenty minutes later, Lorcan stood with an arm around Finnlea's shoulders, watching as the paramedics worked on Liem. A patrol officer stood nearby, his notebook out as he jotted down the statements that Finnlea and Lorcan had given.

Lorcan paced the waiting room, anxious to hear about his brother. Finnlea was curled up in a chair, her arms wrapped around herself. She was praying, he could tell. He sighed before he moved to sit beside her.

"Finnlea? Did Liem say anything?" Lorcan was desperate to know where his brother had been.

"No, he didn't. He hugged, shut the door, and then collapsed." Finnlea rubbed at her elbow where the carpet had rubbed it slightly raw. She rubbed at it without thinking. Her focus was on the officers who moved around the room. Finnlea sighed. They were there to protect her and she hated the loss of her freedom.

Lorcan nodded, having come to the conclusion that Liem had not said anything. His head went back on the wall behind him as he prayed and sought to find the peace in the situation that could only come from God.

Chapter 13

The physician treating Liem studied the X-ray pictures and then the CT pictures. He was puzzled. Liem had a large bruise on his left hip and thigh that was fading. To him, it looked as if Liem had been hit by a vehicle of some sort. Liem had not been awake to confirm that. Liem was still unconscious and he had no idea when the younger man would rouse. The physician turned and asked the nurse to bring in whoever was Liem's next of kin.

Lorcan was on his feet as the nurse approached him. He hesitated before his hand reached for Finnlea's, drawing her with him despite her protests. The physician turned as he heard their footsteps.

"You're the next of kin?" His keen eyes studied the younger people.

"I'm his brother. This is his girlfriend." Lorcan's hand tightened on Finnlea's hand even as he gave a slight shake of his head. That was how Liem was thinking of her. "What is his condition?"

"He hasn't woken yet. I don't know what he's gone through but he has not had the treatment that he needed to receive. Was he struck by a vehicle?"

Lorcan and Finnlea shared a look. That would explain what had happened for him to go off the running track.

"Why do you ask that?" Finnlea's voice was almost inaudible.

"He has a large bruise on his left hip and leg. That's compatible with that."

Lorcan shrugged. They had no idea how Liem had been hurt or where he had been. They stood beside the stretcher. Finnlea's hand rested on Liem's. She was angry and that was something that she needed to give over to God.

Late that night, Lorcan stood from the chair that he had been sitting in. He stretched, watching Finnlea as he did so. Her head was on the pillow near Liem's as she slept. He had found a blanket to cover her. Lorcan knew there was an officer stationed outside of the door.

Walking from the room, Lorcan paced the hallway. The detective who had come around at the news that Liem was in the hospital had stated that he wanted the three of them together, at least until he could get Liem's statement.

Turning as he heard footsteps approaching him, Lorcan was not surprised to see Paul walking towards him. Their pastor, Luke, was with him.

"Lorcan?" Paul pointed to some chairs. "How is Liem?"

Lorcan shrugged, not sure what to say. The physician had been around earlier, not able to provide any answers for them. Lorcan was praying that Liem would awaken and be able to tell them what had happened.

Luke began to pray for the trio, his prayer liberally sprinkled with God's promises. Lorcan could feel himself relaxing as he felt the presence of God surrounding him. His head went back on the wall behind him as he slept.

Luke rose at last and headed for where he could find Liem. The officer nodded at Luke as the minister entered the room.

In the early morning hours, Liem began to stir, his head turning to the side. He felt hair brushing his cheek. His eyes cracked open and he stared at Finnlea. He didn't recognize her. He looked up as a form that loomed nearby.

"Liem?"

Lorcan drew in a deep breath. He was safe, wasn't he? Or were Lorcan and the lady captive as well?

"Liem? Wake up, brother. We need to talk."

"Lorcan? Where am I?"

"In the hospital. Finnlea and I have been worried about you."

"Finnlea? Who's she?" Liem jumped as he felt a slap on his arm.

Finnlea had roused as Lorcan had spoken to Liem. She glared at him, hurt on her face. She ran from the room and just continued to run. Anger flared within her for the time being.

Lorcan watched her run before he turned back to his brother. Liem had sat upright, one arm bracing him that way. The other hand rested on the top of his head. Lorcan was unable to hold back his snicker as he watched his brother.

"Lorcan? Explain. Who was that?" Liem glared at his brother.

"The lady? That's Finnlea. You two shared an adventure. And you are interested in her. She's been trying to find you." Lorcan pulled up a seat and sat.

"An adventure? Explain yourself, Lorcan." Liem raised the head of the bed and leaned back on the pillow.

And Lorcan did just that. Liem's eyes, now clear, never left his brother's face. When Lorcan had finished, Liem looked past him at the door. Throwing back his blankets, he shifted to the side of the bed. He pulled the intravenous line that ran to his hand. He knew that he shouldn't leave but he was driven to find that lady. She had been haunting what waking hours that he had had.

Dressed in clean clothes but struggling to stay upright, Liam headed for the door, Lorcan following him. Liem stalked past the police officer, Lorcan merely shrugging. The police officer was beside Liem, unable to stop him from leaving. The officer called it in as he followed Lorcan's truck as that man headed for Finnlea's home.

Lorcan's hand on his arm helped Liem keep his balance as he slowly lifted one foot after the other to climb the steps to find Finnlea. The officer followed, watchful for anything that was out of place.

———

The early morning sounds echoed in their ears. Liem drew in a deep breath of fresh air. He didn't know he could handle being locked behind a door any more, even if that was his own home.

Chapter 14

Finnlea stared at the entry door, her arms wrapped around her abdomen. She had found another letter taped to her door when she had stumbled to a stop in front of it. She had angrily ripped it down before she was inside and then quietly closing the door behind her. This could not be happening, she decided. They must have the wrong house.

She crept to the door and listened, recognizing Lorcan's voice. She just didn't understand why he was there and not with Liem. Finnlea yanked open the door, shock appearing on her face. She backed away as the others entered the house, the officer pulling the door closed behind them.

"What are you doing here?" Finnlea was not backing down from Liem. She felt Lorcan's hand tighten on her shoulder as he headed past her and for the kitchen to make the coffee that he knew that all needed.

"I had to see you." Liem swayed as he tried to keep his balance. A hand came out to rest against the wall beside him. That was the only thing keeping him on his feet.

Finnlea snorted as she studied him. She sighed before she wrapped an arm around him and turned him to the living room. She heard Lorcan heading for the door and then heard Paul's voice. Finnlea gave a small squeak as Liem pulled her down with him to the couch.

Liem refused to let Finnlea go, feeling that she was his only contact with reality. That wasn't quite true. He began to pray for his memory to come back. Finnlea was a lady whom he wanted to keep as a friend.

Paul handed the couple their mugs of coffee before he took his from Lorcan and then found a seat. His head bowed as Lorcan began to pray.

Liem studied his friend. He knew that he had to give a statement but he really didn't think that he had much of one to give.

"Liem? Talk to me." Paul had come back from his vacation when word had come in that Liem had appeared once more.

Liem nodded, not sure what to say. His arm tightened around Finnlea and prevented Finnlea from moving away from him. That earned him a glare, Lorcan and Paul barely able to hide their amusement.

"I don't remember much, Paul. I woke up a few times but my mind wasn't really clear until yesterday. I could not find any door into the room where I was kept. There had to be a panel of some kind that opened. Other than the artificial light, there was a cheap skylight. I managed to pull the stand from beside the bed under it and could reach it. I managed to break it and pulled myself out onto the roof. It was a garage. I managed to lower myself to the ground. I think it was a farm. I headed away from there. I don't remember how I got to the hospital. And I never saw anyone. I have no idea why I was there."

"You ended up here, Liem." Lorcan spoke up, his eyes watching Finnlea who in turn was watching Liem. He noted the confused look on her face.

"Here? I don't know this place, do I?" Liem was uncertain that Lorcan was telling him the truth.

"You do, Liem. For now, trust us on that." Paul studied his notes. Liem was correct, he decided. And that would not help them solve this adventure. All he could do was pray for his friends.

Paul rose at last and let himself out. He nodded at the officer who was stationed at the do. He turned for a moment, knowing that the other tenants had been interviewed. At some point, he would interview them again.

Lorcan had risen as well and searched for food for the three of them. It was obvious that Liem had no intention of letting go of Finnlea any time soon.

Finnlea had finally relaxed somewhat against Liem. She watched him closely, seeing the fatigue on his face. She also knew that he would not leave her.

"Finnlea? We are friends?" Liem's voice was hesitant as he asked the question that he had to ask.

"We are, Liem. You've been trying to protect me." Finnlea gave brief history of what had happened, leaving Liem staring at her in shock.

"That never happened."

"Trust me. It did. And now those men are going to be looking for you. They know that you've escaped. I had a letter on my door that they want you. I just don't know why."

68

"To get to you, Finnlea. They know that Liem would find you." Lorcan set down the tray of food that he was carrying. "Liem, you won't be working for a while. I can work from anywhere. Let's keep you two together at Finnlea's store."

Liem didn't respond. He slept with his arm tight around his lady. Lorcan gave a grin before he shifted Liem to stretch out on the couch, Finnlea helping him before she slipped to a seating position beside the couch.

"Lorcan? Should he be here?"

"Not likely, Finnlea. He needed to see you. At the moment, he doesn't really remember you. Subconsciously, he knows you and is driven to be with you."

"But that puts him in danger." Finnlea was desperate to send Liem away. Only she knew that would not work.

"He's not going anywhere, Finnlea. He'll be there with you. If you force him to stay away, he'll be there in the shadow, keeping watch over you. And he'll have me there right beside him."

"He will, won't he?" Finnlea knew that Lorcan spoke the truth. "How do we find out who is behind this?"

"That's a good question, Finnlea. Eve is working for you today. If I can use your computer, I'll pull what I have found and go over it with you. You may see something that I missed."

Finnlea nodded.

"Can we pray, Lorcan?"

Chapter 15

Finnlea looked up from the massive amount of paper that Lorcan had handed her. She was shocked at what he had found. He had slipped away just before noon, checking on the store before he had stopped at his own home to grab his laptop and the file folders of information.

"How did you do that again? I didn't know that about my family."

"You have a great ancestry, Finnlea, as do we." Lorcan looked over at Liem. His brother had not roused at all. That worried him enough to call a physician friend who promised to drop around that afternoon.

"Shouldn't Liem be awake?" Finnlea set aside the papers that she was holding to rise and sit on the floor near Liem. Her arm stretched around him.

"A friend will be here soon, Finnlea. Liem is sleeping, Finnlea. We'll see what Rob has to say." Lorcan's attention went back to his paperwork. He had to set aside Finnlea and Liem's investigation for now. He had other investigations that he needed to work on.

Rob tucked away his stethoscope and then reached for the IV line that he had started. He could find little wrong with Liem other than dehydration. That was concerning but the IV would help with that. He rose to his feet, watching Finnlea as he did so. Something was going on with these two. He just wasn't sure what.

Lorcan wasn't sure what Rob's thoughts were. He nodded towards the kitchen, knowing that Finnlea would not leave Liem's side.

"Rob? What can you tell me?"

"Liem's dehydrated for one thing. I don't see anything else. I'll drop off the blood samples on my way. I'll be back this evening to check on him." Rob walked away, leaving Lorcan staring after him.

Finnlea approached him, reaching past him to pour them mugs of coffee. She didn't speak, just hugged the man whom she now considered to be a brother before she walked to her office to call Eve. To hear that all was well at the store was a relief. God had provided for her and she was grateful for that. She had not expected the store to take off as it had.

Luke had appeared by the time she returned to the living room. He was someone whom she was grateful for as well. He had prayed for them and then left. A piece of paper was dropped on the coffee table. It contained a list of God's promises of protection and peace. Finnlea was grateful for that.

Finnlea's head went down against Liem's arm as she slept. She just could not stay awake. Lorcan gave a sad smile as he sat down nearby. The letter that Finnlea had found on her door was just more threats that really didn't say much.

Liem roused in the early evening, a hand rubbing at his face. He frowned as he looked around. It was not his home. He looked down at the arm over him before his hand rested on Finnlea's head. He felt a connection with the lady. He just could not remember her.

Lorcan was there to help his brother sit up and then to lift Finnlea to the couch. He covered her before he sat on the coffee table.

"Liem?" Lorcan's voice held a question that had his brother nodding.

"I'm okay, Lorcan. I just need to clean up." Liem struggled to his feet, swaying for a moment.

"I grabbed some of your stuff. The bathroom is down the hall on your right." Lorcan watched his brother walk away from him. He wouldn't be working just yet. Thankfully friends had stepped in for him.

Liem walked back through the house to the kitchen. He felt better now that he had showered, shaved, and in clean clothes. He reached to pour a mug of coffee and then leaned over the pot of soup that was simmering on the stove. Liem realized that he was starving. Heading for the living room, he found a seat where he could watch Finnlea. He sighed. She seemed to be important to him. Memories were tickling at the edge of his mind.

Finnlea stirred, feeling someone watching her. She sat up and pushed back the hair that had fallen over her face. She jumped as she saw Liem sitting nearby and watching her.

"Liem?" Her voice was tentative as she said his name.

"Finnlea?" Liem gave a quick grin as she glared at him. "You needed that sleep."

Finnlea nodded before she was on her feet and walking from the room. Liem's head turned as he watched her before he too was on his feet to follow her.

"Where's Lorcan?" Finnlea's voice broke through the silence.

"He's outside. Just for a moment." Liem took the bowls of soup as Finnlea filled them and placed them on the table. He waited for her to choose a chair before he sat and reached for her hand. His prayer filled the room.

Finnlea studied Liem as they ate, not sure what to say. She sighed to herself. She just knew that he would try and protect her. She wasn't sure that she wanted that.

Liem had been gone for hours before the panel to the room slid open. The man stared first in disbelief and then in consternation at the empty room. Liem had disappeared. He stared up at the skylight, wondering how Liem had managed to break the glass. The man turned and shoved the panel shut. He needed to find his boss but that was a conversation that he was not looking forward to having.

Chapter 16

The man's employer stared at him in disbelief before the disbelief changed to anger and rage. There should have been no way that Liem should have been able to escape. He would find him once more and lock him away in a room that he could not escape from. He had monitored Finnlea's activities and knew that Liem seemed to be important to her. He sent the man away with orders to find Liem and imprison him again.

Finnlea walked towards her store the next morning. She needed to be there. Lorcan had to literally drag Liem away the night before. She knew that he would turn up at some point over the day. Finnlea was not sure how to feel about that. He would begin to hover and she definitely did not want that.

Paul stood on Liem's front porch, locked in a stare down with his friend. He was not backing down from Liem. He needed to interview him again whether or not Liem was willing to do that.

"Liem? We do need to talk soon. Finnlea is okay. I have an officer on duty there." Paul pointed back into Liem's house. "Inside and now." He could feel the prickles on the back of his neck that meant someone was out there and monitoring Liem and his movements.

"Paul?" Lim backed up as Paul entered and shut and locked the door behind him.

"Liem? Someone is out there and watching you. It is only a matter of time before you disappear

---

75

again. If that happens, you may never be seen again. They will not hesitate to kill you. Do you understand that?"

Liem nodded slowly. Lorcan had said the very same thing that morning before he left. Liem understood only too well what the men were saying. For now, he was stuck at home until he replaced his truck and the tools that had disappeared as well. Lorcan had promised to take him truck shopping that afternoon.

"I get that, Paul. What can you tell me?"

"Not a lot, unfortunately, Liem. We don't know where you were held. You can't remember."

"No, I can't and I need to." Liem blew out a breath. "What can you tell me?"

Paul nodded. Liem was asking the question that Paul knew that he would. He began to speak and laid it all out for him. Not that there was a lot to say. Liem stared at Paul with a worried look in his eyes.

"How do we do this, Paul? How do we keep Finnlea safe?"

"Date her, Liem. For the time being, be seen around town. Whoever it is that is behind this? They already see you as a couple." Paul knew what he was asking Liem to do. His reading of his friend was that Liem was interested in Finnlea.

"I see. Somehow, I don't know that it would work. She and Lorcan seem like a couple." Liem could not say anything more.

"They react with one another like brother and sister. Lorcan sees that you're interested in her. He's not interested in her in a romantic way. Finnlea is interested in seeing where you two head. She's cautious that way, Liem. Tread carefully with her. She hasn't shared her past with us. You know that we have dug into that as well as your own. It's what we do."

Liem nodded. He knew that Paul would have done that but he also knew that Paul would not share that information with either one of them unless he had to.

"So, Paul? What next? We have to live our lives. We can't hide."

Paul was shaking his head as Liem finished.

"No, you can't hide. You go about your daily lives. You find another truck, replace your tools, and go back to work. You are seen out and about with Finnlea. And I can guarantee that she will fight you on that. She's been quiet in the last few days just because she was worried about you. And that has suppressed her personality. Expect it to come back." Paul looked down at his notes before he studied his friend. He could see the changes that showed on his face.

Finnlea locked the door to her store with a sigh. It had been one of those busy days. She had felt overrun with customers and was not eager to drive home. Finnlea walked towards her car, stopping abruptly as she saw sneakers in her line of sight. She looked up to see Liem grinning at her.

"What are you doing here?" She glared at him as his grin widened.

"To find you." He reached for her keys, taking them gently from her hand.

"Go home, Liem. You shouldn't be here."

"I have to be. Paul told me to."

Finnlea snorted. She just could not see Paul doing that. She glared at Liem as he continued to grin at her.

"He did do just that. He told me that we needed to be seen together. In fact, Paul told me to date you."

"He did no such thing." Finnlea stared at Liem in shock. "He wouldn't do that."

"Sorry, but he did." Liem swung an arm around her, nudging her forward and to the passenger side of her car. "Hop in, beautiful. I want to take you out for a meal."

Finnlea refused to move, glaring at Liem.

"Go home, Liem."

"I can't. I don't have a vehicle." Paul had dropped him off. Liem knew that he could call Lorcan and get him to pick him up. He just didn't want to.

Finnlea continued to refuse to move. Her eyes didn't leave his face. She felt the eyes watching them and grew fearful before the promises of protection from God flooded her mind.

"We can't do this, Liem. I don't want you hurt again or have you disappear."

Liem reached to hug her, feeling the shudders of fear wracking er.

"I would rather it be me than you. I can handle myself."

Neither one of the couple looked around as they heard a truck draw up beside them. Lorcan was grinning as he observed the standoff. He figured that Finnlea would win and that he would be giving his brother a ride home.

"Where are we eating, Liem? And is Lorcan coming too?" Finnlea sounded both disgruntled and resigned to the fact that she would be eating with the brothers.

Lorcan began to laugh, knowing that Liem really hadn't won. Finnlea had just decided to go along with them.

"We'll find a spot." Liem gave her a hug before he tucked her into the car. "And I would like it if you went truck shopping with us." Liem walked around the car to the driver's side, catching Lorcan's wide grin.

Chapter 17

That following Saturday, Finnlea stood in her store, listening to Eve speaking with a customer. It had been a busy day and she was exhausted. It was the worry and stress of the situation that was driving that. The uncertainty of who it was as well was playing with her mind. She was trying hard to cling to every promise of God that she could find.

Sending Eve on her way, Finnlea locked up and headed for her car. She was watchful, her head moving as she searched the area around her store. She knew that she was being watched. For once, Liem had not shown up. Finnlea breathed a sigh of relief. She was worried about him. Whoever was after her had targeted Liem just to get to her. Heading for her home, Finnlea ran for her house and locked herself inside it. Having to lock herself away all the time was making her short-tempered. At least today, she thought, she had not found a letter on her door. Those were appearing every other day. That worried Finnlea as she worried about her fellow tenants.

Liem stared at Finnlea's store. She had already left and that disappointed him. He had been delayed picking up his new truck and had not reached her store in time to follow her home. He turned back to his truck, unwilling to abandon the store even though Finnlea had already left for the day. Liem knew that he needed give her space. He just didn't want to.

Hearing his name called, Liem turned seeing Paul and Lorcan walking towards him.

"Liem? Do you have time for a coffee?" Paul grinned at his friend even as he saw the lines that now seemed to be a part of his face. They needed to solve this with Finnlea and soon.

'I do." Liem pointed to the nearby coffee shop. "Does that work?"

The three men were soon seated in the coffeeshop with a meal in front of them. Conversation was light and skipped through many topics. Paul wrapped his hands around his mug, his eyes on Liem.

"Liem? How are you really doing?"

Liem shrugged, not sure what to say. He wasn't sure how he felt. Lorcan watched the conflicting emotions that chased one another across his brother's face.

"How close are you to moving this?" Liem kept his eyes steady on Paul.

"Not where we want to be, Liem. We just don't have enough information to solve it. The information is trickling in. Not one person has given us what we need." Paul was frustrated at that.

Liem found his favourite wicker chair on his back deck late that evening. He listened the night sounds that surrounded him. It was a favourite time of day for him, finding it a time just to relax and spend time with his Lord. He had not been able to do that for a few days.

Lorcan looked around the church the next morning. He could see neither Liem nor Finnlea. He walked rapidly away from the building and found his truck. He parked outside of his brother's house and then ran for the front door. He let himself in and searched for Liem. Lorcan paused as he found Liem on the couch in the living room, sound asleep.

Nodding his head, Lorcan headed for the kitchen to make coffee. The vibrating of his phone caught his attention. He read the message from Finnlea. She sounded somewhat panicked at not being able to get in touch with Liem. Lorcan smiled as he sent back a quick response. Yes, he decided, there was unrest on both sides. And he would do what he could to further that budding romance.

A quiet tap at the door had Lorcan heading that way. Finnlea stood there, worry on her face.

"Lorcan? You're sure that he's okay?" Finnlea dropped her purse on the table in the entryway.

"He is, Finnlea." Lorcan pointed to the living room. "He's in there, Go on in. I have coffee and muffins ready."

Finnlea nodded, not really hearing what he said. She stood for a moment, just watching Liem as he slept. She was seated beside him, an arm around him, when Lorcan appeared. The tray that he carried hit the coffee table before he found his own seat. He watched his brother and then Finnlea before he nodded. They were falling in love with one another, he decided, and they suited one another.

Liem roused at last, sensing that he was not alone. He cracked open one eye to see Lorcan deep in concentration on his laptop. A soft sound caught at his ear. He turned his head to come almost nose to nose with Finnlea. That lady had not moved from where she had planted herself on the floor earlier.

Liem reached to touch her cheek before he sat up, drawing her up beside him. He squinted at the clock and groaned. None of them had made it to church that day. He had needed to be there.

Lorcan looked as Liem stirred, a frown on his face for a moment. He set aside his laptop to one side.

"Liem, Are you okay?" Lorcan was really beginning to worry about his brother.

Liem shrugged. He had no idea how he was to feel.

"How long have you been here?"

"Around three hours or so. I was here when Finnlea arrived. She just sat down on the floor beside you and then slept." Lorcan was out into the kitchen and then returned with coffee and fresh muffins. "How long did you sleep?"

Liem squinted at the clock even as he reached for a muffin. He then shrugged. He wasn't quite sure himself how long it had been.

"I don't know. Since around ten last night." Liem looked down at Finnlea. "She's still sleeping?"

"She is." Lorca grinned at his brother. "You are both wearing out."

"We are. And there doesn't seem to be any sign of it ending."

Chapter 18

A week passed. Finnlea was growing more and more frustrated with the lack of progress that was being made in the investigation. She called Paul every day. It had come to the point that Paul was beginning to just answer his phone with the comment that he was still working on it when he knew it was her calling him.

Liem watched Finnlea as much as she would let him. She would frown at him and then send him away. He would grin and then hug her. He would walk away only to turn up again the next day. Lorcan was often with him. He had told Liem that he wanted to see who would win. He grinned as he stated that he was sure that it would be Finnlea. Finnlea had told Lorcan to go find something to investigate. He had continued to laugh as he walked away.

That Sunday Finnlea stood and stared at the package that sat on the sidewalk at the foot of the door. She wrapped her arms around herself, finding that she was shaking in fear. She backed up into the house and slammed the door shut before she locked it. Her phone was in her hand as Finnlea called Paul. Paul was not surprised to hear that she had received a package.

Paul stood beside the crime scene tech as she sorted through the photos. And there were many. Paul had lost count of them. They covered a number of years. He shot a look at the house door and then back at the photo that he held. It was a photo of Finnlea at what he could only assume was from her high school graduation. That disturbed him greatly. This meant that whoever was after her had been stalking her for years. This had just expanded his investigation.

Finnlea turned from the front window as Paul tapped at the door and then entered. She watched as he carefully closed the door behind him.

"Paul?"

Finnlea's voice brought his eyes to her. He sighed to himself. He had no way of knowing how she would react to what was in the box. Paul took time to pray for her.

"Finnlea? Can we sit? I need to go over what was in the box. I just don't want to pick you up off the floor." Paul grinned at her. Only his grin did not reach his eyes.

"You're scaring me, Paul. I don't like that." Finnlea found a seat, her eyes watchful as Paul too sat. "Again, what was in that box?"

"Photos, Finnlea. Photos of you over the years. There seems to be one for every month since your high school graduation. Who do you know would do that?"

Finnlea paled at Paul's words. Then it was true after all. She had felt followed for years. She had gone to the authorities on one occasion but had felt rebuffed by the officer that she had spoken to. There had just not been any sign of what she had stated to them.

"For all those years? But why? I don't understand it. I had gone to the police a few years ago but they said that they could not investigate as there was no evidence of anyone following me."

Paul grew angry. He knew that was likely the case. It just frustrated him that it had come to the point that it had

"You have felt followed?"

Finnlea nodded before she was on her feet. Paul could hear the sound of the printer before Finnlea was back beside him, handing him a stack of paper.

"These are my notes. If I could see the photos, I could tell you where they were taken and if they matched up to any of these places."

Paul nodded. They would need Finnlea's input. He just hated to put her through that.

"Let our team do what they need to. Then, I'll have you come down and we'll go through them together. We'll need a couple of days."

Two days later, Finnlea stood in a conference room, staring at the copies of the photos that were placed on a number of tables. It unnerved her to see how many that there were. She had not expected to see that many.

Liem stood tight beside her, an arm around her. He had given her no option whether he was there or not. He had to be there to protect his lady. Finnlea had stared at him in disbelief when he had reached for her hand and tried to tug it away from his. He had grinned at the disgruntled look that she shot at him. Liem was well aware that she wanted to stand on her own two feet and was ready to tell him to leave her alone, Only Finnlea didn't. She simply turned to Paul and demanded to see the photos. Liem had stared at her and then at Paul, barely hiding his grin.

Paul stood just inside the door, reading from a folder before he looked up and caught sight of Liem standing beside Finnlea. He caught the hint of the sight of a knight of old standing strong and true beside the lady of his dreams, ready to defend and protect her. He shook his head to clear the image.

"Paul? There are this many?" Finnlea was aghast at the volume of photos.

"There are. As far as we can tell, however it is has taken a photo or two every month. We think it starts when you graduated from high school." Paul watched with sympathy as her face crumpled and then tightened.

Finnlea reached for the marker that Paul was handing her. She walked the lengths of the tables, studying each picture. She reached to move each one into correct chronological order. She paused for a moment, staring the very first picture.

"What do you want me to do?" Her voice shook with the strength of her emotions.

"Write the date on the photo if you can remember the date. If not, then the month and year are good. And the location as well." Paul turned as Liem moved to stand beside Finnlea.

"This is taking a lot from her. She's losing who she is under the weight of it all." Liem was worried about her. "And you know that she will want copies."

———

Paul nodded. He had discussed that with his supervisor. They had agreed to give her a copy of the photos but only if she asked for them.

Chapter 19

Liem wrapped an arm around her as she stood and stared down at the very last photo. It had been taken just the week before as the couple had walked towards Lorcan in a nearby parking lot. Finnlea was suddenly deeply afraid. She spun to wrap her arms around Liem, his arms coming around her. She was afraid, he knew, and yet he had no way of knowing how to make it all better. He wanted to be her protector but knew that God was that.

Finnlea shoved away from Liem and stalked towards Paul, A furious look on her face. She planted herself in front of him, hands on her hips. Paul had to bite his smile even as he realized that Finnlea was not only angry but deeply afraid. And he had no answers to give her that would help to resolve that. They were really not that close to solving this investigation.

"Paul?" Finnlea waited for him to speak as she continued to scowl at him.

Paul gently turned her back to face the tables. He watched Liem as he did so, knowing that Liem wanted to step in with Finnlea yet knowing that he could not.

"You've marked everything for us?" Paul's voice was quiet.

"I have, Paul. I just don't understand this. There is at least one photo for each month for years. Sometimes two or three. It goes back to when I was

---

89

eighteen. Did whoever it was take pictures before then and not give them to me?"

"I would suspect that they waited until you were an adult."

Finnlea nodded, having come to that conclusion.

"I want copies of these, Paul. I want to go over each one." Finnlea looked up when Paul did not respond. "Did you hear me? I want copies."

"And we have copies for you. The only condition is that you talk to us about what you discover on them."

Paul watched from the sidewalk in front of the police detachment as Finnlea and Liem walked away. Her hand was tight in Liem's. He had dropped the packages of photos into a backpack that Lorcan now had over his shoulder. Paul shook his head. The brothers were trying hard to protect her. Yet Finnlea had to feel smothered. He wondered how long it would take for her to tell them off.

Finnlea paced her house in the early morning hours the next morning. To say that she was petrified with fear was an understatement. She eyed the bundles of photos. Finnlea knew that she needed to go over them again but was afraid to. She was also certain that both Liem and Lorcan wanted to do the same. She just wanted her mom and dad and they weren't there.

A noise at her door a few hours later roused her. She opened it to stare at Liem as he stood there in front of her. Backing away from him, she scowled at him.

Of course, he would show up, now wouldn't he? Finnlea looked past him at the older lady who had followed him into her house. She had no idea who she was. Liem continued to grin as he wrapped Finnlea into a hug before he turned to face the other lady and Lorcan who had by now appeared.

"Finnlea, this is our Aunt Lora. She is just back from a trip. When she heard what was happening, she insisted that she had to meet you." Liem stepped to one side, almost pushed that way by his aunt.

Lora didn't stand on formalities. She just reached to hug Finnlea, a prayer whispering in the younger lady's ears. Her hug was just so much like her mother's and aunt's that Finnlea broke down in tears. The two men moved past the ladies towards the kitchen.

Finnlea stepped back after a few minutes, embarrassed that she had broken down. It had all come to a head and the comfort that Lora offered had broken through her reserves. Finnlea had spoken with two of her aunts the night before but they were hours away from her and that really hadn't helped.

"I know these boys have sprung me on you. You look as if you needed a hug or two."

"Thank you. It does help." Finnlea studied Lora, thankful that God had answered a plea from her heart and brought a lady into her life. "Liem and Lorcan do try but sometimes you just need to talk with another lady." Finnlea swiped at her face. "I don't have my mom and I need her."

"Of course, you do." Lora turned Finnlea towards her bedroom. "Go and get yourself back together. I'll corral those two and rescue your kitchen." Lora grinned at Finnlea before she sent her down the hall with a gentle shove. She felt an arm around her shoulders and a kiss on her cheek.

Liem stood beside his aunt, grateful for how she had reached out to Finnlea. He could only do so much but Lora reached through to Finnlea as he knew that she would.

"Thanks, Aunt Lora. She's needed a mother figure and hasn't had one here."

Lora hugged her nephew and then went to find Lorcan. Liem simply leaned against the wall as he waited for Finnlea, praying for his lady. He looked up as he heard soft movement and simply opened his arms. Finnlea ran toward him, finding comfort in his tight hug. She was falling in love with the tall, handsome man who was trying so hard to protect her. She didn't know that Liem had already decided that he was in love with her.

Lora watched her nephew and his lady, knowing that Liem was working up the courage to tell her that. All she could do was pray for them.

"Liem? Let's eat. Then, we'll spend some time in prayer. Finnlea, I'm curious to see those photos. Will you share them?"

"I will and gladly. I don't like it that someone has been stalking me like this." Finnlea's face was clouded with fear and worry.

"We will do that, Finnlea." Lorcan watched her closely, a frown on his face.

"Yeah, well. We'll see how well that works."

An hour later, Finnlea was on her feet and headed for her office to find the bundles of photos. She paused, frowning for a moment. She was sure that she had felt a hand on her head. Only there was no one else in the room.

Chapter 20

Liem rose from where he had been sitting to pace. To see the extent of the stalking was disturbing to say the least. Someone had been following Finnlea no matter where she went or what she faced. He paused for a moment, trying to think through the implications of what the photos showed. Was it just simply stalking or something more sinister?

Lorcan had been compiling the statistics from what Finnlea had been remembering. She had simply begun to talk about the places where the photos had been taken. Lora was recording Finnlea's words, planning on transcribing them. She watched the younger lady closely. She was worried about Finnlea.

Finnlea rose at last, stretching and then walking outside to the back deck. She needed some fresh air and only being outside would help. She heard the door open and close behind her and then felt Liem's arms around her. She leaned back against him. The tumult within her eased to some extent.

Liem began to talk, just about nothing really important. He told her about his parents, how he had been raised. He talked about his dreams. He then began to talk about his dream lady. Liem felt Finnlea tense in his arms and knew that she was ready to run.

"You are that lady, Finnlea. I just wanted you to know that." Liem dropped a kiss on her temple and then turned to walk back inside the house. He sat at the table, reaching for the papers that Lorcan was handing him. He didn't see the look that Lorcan and Lora exchanged.

Lorcan rose some minutes later, heading outside to find Finnlea. He had a photo in his hand that he had questions about. He sat in a wicker chair near to where Finnlea had curled up on a wicker loveseat. She watched him without saying a word.

Lorcan stared down at the photo. It had been taken approximately five years previously. Instead of asking Finnlea about it, he began to quote Bible verses about peace, protection, and defense. He was confident that God was in control of it all. He was the One who was the protector.

Finnlea reached at last for the photo, her finger tracing the house that was in it

"This was my maternal grandparents' house. This photo was taken the day the new owners took possession. They were gracious enough to let us walk through it one last time." Her voice was sober. "This photo? I had stepped outside just to gather my emotion. Who does this?" She felt Liem sit beside her and simply reach for her hand. She sighed. "Are we making any sense of it?"

"Not yet, but we will." Liem was determined to solve it. He just knew that it would not be that day. "You're in the store tomorrow and I have to work."

"I know. I should have been there today. Eve told me to stay home." Finnlea was growing discouraged. She just didn't know how to pull herself out it.

The next day, Liem reached for his hammer, pausing for a moment. He too was discouraged. It didn't seem as if they were making any progress with their search. Paul had been non-committal about the investigation. Paul could also not tell Liem much about his own abduction. And there had been no word on his truck. Liem resented having to replace it and everything that was in it. One thing that had puzzled all of them was that Liem's phone had not been taken from him.

Lora walked through Finnlea's store, recognizing many of the artists. Finnlea had created a space that had not existed before, a place that had been badly needed. She stood and watched Finnlea interact with the customers. She has a knack, Lora decided, in finding just the piece of art that the customer was looking for. Lora frowned. She just did not understand why someone was going after Finnlea. Nothing that they had discovered or that Finnlea had remembered had led to a conclusion.

Finnlea moved around her store, content for the moment. She knew that it wouldn't last. She looked up to find Lora standing in front of her, a mug of tea extended towards her.

"Thank you, Lora. I need this." Finnlea took it gratefully. "You've been here all day."

"I have been, Finnlea. You have a wonderful store. I left a list on your desk of others who have heard of your store and are interested in speaking with you." Lora looked around. "You're getting busier here."

"I am. I never expected theatre to take off as it has. I am also getting requests for a website and online store."

Lora grinned at that.

"That's where I come in. I can set up a website for you and an online store. I have retired from my government job and am still too young to be considered retired."

Finnlea looked at her in surprise. God had just provided for her with someone who could help expand her dream.

"Then, thank you. I would need to contact each artisan and determine which ones are willing to do that." Finnlea reached to hug Lora. "God is here, isn't He?"

"He is, Finnlea. He has never left you. Now, it's close to closing time. How be you close shop and come home with me for a meal? I have never been a mother and I will not replace yours. Can you look at me as a concerned older friend?"

Finnlea continued to stare at Lora before she nodded. A short time later, she was walking into Lora's home, not surprised that she lived a block down from her house on her own street. She looked up for a moment, whispering a quiet thank you to God.

Chapter 21

Backing up until he could not move any further, Liem's hands were raised and fisted. He didn't know the three men who now surrounded him in a half-circle. He knew that if he was attacked, he would not be able to defend himself at all.

"Where is she?" The older of the men finally spoke.

"Where's who?" Liem had a good idea that they were looking for Finnlea. Right now though, he had no idea where she was. He had simply stopped at a local hardware store to make a purchase. He had not expected to find anyone waiting for him. He prayed, asking that God protect his lady.

"You know who. Your woman." The man watched dispassionately as Liem stared back at him without speaking.

Liem was unable to avoid the hard knotted fist that landed in his abdomen. Held upright by the hands of two of the men, he struggled to breathe. Dark spots danced in front of his eyes. A few minutes, Liem crumpled to the ground. His eyes closed as he fought to keep concious but lost the battle.

An hour later, Liem struggled to sit upright. He blinked as he tried to clear his vision. He rose cautiously to his feet and then walked towards his truck, an arm wrapped around his abdomen. He stared at the seat before he crawled up onto it and then drove away. Parking in his driveway, his eyes closed before he once more squinted through slitted eyes. Locking the door behind him, Liem dropped his keys on the table and then shuffled towards his bedroom. He dropped facedown on the bed, once more losing his fight to stay awake.

Lorcan stared at his phone, a frown on his face. Liem had not shown up at his home to have a Friday night supper. To not call his brother or answer any texts was not Liem. Lorcan turned to bundle up the meal and then run for his truck. He parked beside Liem's truck and then was out of his own truck and running for the house. Entering, he called for Liem, worry for his brother driving him to search the house. Lorcan stood over his brother, staring down at him. Something had happened, he deduced, before he was pulling off Liem's work boots and covering him with a blanket.

Walking back out to his truck, Lorcan retrieved his laptop and their dinner. The dinner went into the fridge before he found a seat in the living room. He was not leaving until Liem was on his feet and could explain what had happened to him. And he could do nothing else but pray for his brother.

It was early morning before Liem rolled to his side, rubbing at his abdomen. He grimaced at the pain that caused. On his feet, he rummaged through his dresser for clean clothes and then stumbled to the bathroom where he showered and shaved. He stared in dismay at the bruises on his body and sighed. Liem knew that he would need to speak with the police. He would do that but not at present.

Stumbling down the hallway, Liem paused at the spare bedroom, seeing his brother asleep in there. He frowned. He had not heard Lorcan coming in.

A mug of fresh coffee in his hand, Liem headed for his office. He stared at his computer before he reached for his Bible. He needed that God time. He looked around ages later to see Lorcan sitting nearby.

"Lorcan?"

"You didn't show up for supper last night. You were crashed on your bed when I found you. What happened?" Lorcan sipped at his coffee, patiently waiting for his brother to respond.

Liem rubbed at the face. He couldn't remember a lot of what happened.

"I'm not really sure, Lorcan. I don't remember what I did after I drove away from the jobsite. I think that I headed for the hardware store but I don't know that I ever reached it." Liem felt at his abdomen. "I was beaten, that much I know."

Lorcan reached for Liem's keys as he walked out of the front door. He searched the truck, finding the tool that Liem had purchased. He stood for a moment staring at the truck before he was searching it. He walked back onto the house, dropping the items on the desk in front of Liem.

Liem stared at the objects before he poked at them. He wasn't quite sure what to make of them.

"Those are trackers, Liem. Someone really wanted to know exactly where you were all the time."

"I see. And we don't know who or why."

"And I need to search Finnlea's car." Lorcan's face was stern.

"We do." Liem squinted at the clock on the shelf above the fireplace. It was too early to find Finnlea. He reached for his phone and shot off a quick text to Paul. That man would be in touch with him when he could.

The two brothers set aside the mystery and began instead to discuss the way that God protected His children.

Chapter 22

Standing on her driveway, Finnlea scowled at Lorcan as he searched around her car. That scowl was next turned to Liem who was searching around her house. Paul next came under her scrutiny as he walked towards her. Lora watched with an amused look on her ace. She thanked God that Finnlea was in Liem's life. He was starting to become less rigid and Finnlea was the reason why.

"Just what are you looking for?"

"These." Lorcan held up to trackers which he dropped into an evidence bag that Paul was holding open. "Liem had them on his truck."

"He did? Who put them there?" Finnlea continued to cowl at the three men. She then sighed. "Liem, what did you find?"

"What I think are cameras. Paul, come with me." Liem and Paul walked away despite Finnlea's protest that he show her what he had found.

Finnlea stomped after the two men, leaving Lorcan and Lora sharing an amused look. She stared at the cameras that the two men were dropping into evidence bags. She was shocked, to say the least.

"How many are there?"

Paul looked around at her, seeing the shock and horror on her face. He hesitated for a moment before he walked away to lock the bags into the trunk of his car, His hand rested on the closed lid for a moment as he digested what had happened to Liem the previous night and what Lorcan and Liem had found. Unfortunately, it did not surprise him. Paul was just not sure how to approach Finnlea about the discoveries.

Late that night, Finnlea cowered in her office, her eyes on the drape-covered windows. She could hear the sounds outside that were not caused by the wind. She covered her head with her arms and began to quote all the verses that stated God was in control. Finnlea could feel His presence in the room with her. Angry at herself, Finnlea was on her feet and walking rapidly through her home. Enough was enough, she decided and reached for the large flashlight that she kept by the back door.

Finnlea flicked on the outside lights and headed outside. Her flashlight lit up the night as she walked around the house and then back inside. She didn't see the two men who stood in the shadows and watched her. They had orders to replace the cameras and make enough noise to frighten her. They had just not expected Finnlea to appear outside to search for the source of the noise that she had heard.

Liem stared at Finnlea the next morning, horror and shock on his face. She stared at him from the opposite side of her store counter.

"You did what? Tell me that you really didn't go outside your own!" Liem was horrified at the thought that she had done just that.

"Of course, I did! What else would I do?" Her words were spit at him, anger sparking from her.

"Call the police? Call me?" Liem's words spit right back at her.

The two stood facing one another in a standoff. Eve moved Finnlea to one side so that she could take care of a customer, an amused look lurking in her eyes. Neither was backing down from one another.

Lora moved in on her nephew, her eyes on Paul who stood behind Liem, not sure about what had walked in on.

"Paul, Finnlea had people around her house last night. She went outside on her own to search."

Paul stared at her and then shook his head. Of course, she would do just that. He knew that God was in control. Paul just wished God's timeline would move a little quicker.

"Finnlea?" Paul waited until she glared at him. "Did you find anything?"

"Other than the gardens destroyed? No, I want this over and now." Finnlea's voice was staccato-like.

Paul grinned at her. He knew that was her wish. It was just one that he could not grant, not yet at this point.

Liem moved away, heading outside and then across to the coffee shop. He needed to walk away from Finnlea for a few minutes. Lorcan followed his brother, pointing to a table outside while he headed inside to grab their beverages. Liem waved at acquaintances as they came and went. Lorcan set the cups on the table and sat across from Liem. He simply waited.

Liem rubbed at his cheek. He was still sore from his beating and had no answers as to why. He had discussed it at length with both Lorcan and Paul. They had not been able to reach any consensus as to why or who. The only thing that they had been able to determine was that Finnlea had to be a part of it

Finnlea watched Liem walk away, knowing that they did indeed need space from one another. He was beginning to hover. She was not used to that and wasn't sure how to feel. She could feel God beginning to work in her heart and loosen the constraints that surrounded it. Finnlea had fallen in love but she didn't know how Liem felt.

"Finnlea?" Paul waited patiently for Finnlea to turn to him. He watched as she needlessly tidied the cards beside her before his hand rested on hers. "I'll head that way and take a walk around your house."

Finnlea looked at him, a disturbed look on her face.

"You can't do that! You're off duty."

"I know, Finnlea. It's okay. Lora drove you this morning. I'll check her car before I leave." Paul walked away, not seeing the look that Finnlea shot after him.

Chapter 23

A week later, Finnlea walked through the local grocery store, her mind not really on her shopping. Because of that, she had been forced to retrace her steps numerous times. She finally loaded the bags containing her groceries into the trunk of her car and drove towards her home. Finnlea stopped her car down the street from her home, suddenly afraid. Something or someone waited for her.

Thirty minutes late, a patrol officer approached her. She had kept herself locked inside her vehicle. She lowered the window as he stopped beside it.

"Finnlea? It's a good thing that you didn't go any further. There's a bomb on your back deck. We also found someone waiting to kidnap you. The bomb squad is on its way. Do you have somewhere that you can wait?"

Finnlea nodded, knowing that Lora was home and that she could go there.

"I do. It's just that I have groceries that I need to put away."

The officer grinned at her.

"Pop open the trunk. I'll put your perishables away for you. Where will you be?"

Finnlea gave the address down the street and then shouldered her purse. She was close to tears. This could not be happening to her. She didn't notice the officer who paced beside her. Lora did and raised her eyebrows. She reached to draw Finnlea into her house and then to a seat in the sunroom.

Finnlea looked at Lora.

"Where's God?"

"He's right here, Finnlea. He has not moved away from you. He has promised not to do that. And God never breaks His promise. He promises to protect and hide you. However, He has not promised that we will have an easy life. He promises that He will walk through it with us. Sometimes, like now, it seems very dark. This is one of those storms that He can calm. At times, He lets the storms rage and calms us."

Finnlea nodded. It was what she had been taught. It didn't help that she knew that she had faced storms before. This time was different. This time? It involved others and that scared her. She didn't want to see anyone seriously hurt or killed because of her. That was what scared her the most, that one of her friends would face that fate.

The man stood openly near the sidewalk across the street from Finnlea's home. He watched with interest as the emergency personnel moved around doing their investigation. Finnlea was running, he decided, and grinned maliciously. She would make a mistake and that would be when he act.

Finnlea paced Lora's front porch, her eyes focused down the street. The patrol officer had appeared a short time before just to speak with her. He reassured her that she could go home soon. He would be back for her once the scene was cleared.

Liem stared at Finnlea the next morning as she stood outside the church. He had had to be out of town the day before and had not spoken with her.

"Did you say a bomb?"

"I did. I couldn't drive up to the house. The officer sent me away. I didn't get home until early this morning." Finnlea blinked, disturbed at the anger that crossed Liem's face. "I didn't call you. There was nothing that you could do." Finnlea walked away from Liem before he ran after her.

His hand reached for hers as he walked beside her. He tucked her into his truck, having heard from Lora that she had driven Finnlea to church that morning. Lora also told him that Finnlea had had an incident the night before that he needed to talk to her about.

"Liem? Just what are you doing? I want to be in church."

"I know that you do. So do I. Humour me. Tell me more about yesterday."

"There is nothing more to tell. I spent the time with Lora before I went home. I am tired of all this. I want my life back." She glared at the scenery outside of the truck. "And it doesn't look as if that is going to happen any time soon."

"No, it isn't. And I want that for you too. I want to date you, Finnlea, and this is getting in the way of me doing that." Liem drove into a coffee shop parking lot and then into the drive-through. He handed her the tray of beverages and the bag of food before he drove away. He headed for the spot that always seemed to bring him peace, a park on a local river bank.

Finnlea stared at him, finally remembering to snap her mouth close. She didn't believe him. Other men had tried to date her over the years. She had walked away from them. To hear Liem state that he wanted to date her? That had shaken Finnlea. She looked away from him, her hand tightening on the bag of food that she held.

Liem pulled into a parking lot near the river, searching the area before he was pulling Finnlea from the truck. He headed for a favourite rock of his that overlooked the river. It was a flat rock, just high enough to be comfortable to sit on. He spread out the blanket, took the food from Finnlea, and then seated her. He sat beside before he reached for her hands. He simply bowed his head and prayed for his lady.

Chapter 24

Finnlea raised her head, feeling safe for a moment. She knew that wouldn't last for long. Whoever it was that was after her would make sure of that.

Liem watched her closely, content to just share a meal with her. The morning was warm, the sunshine brilliant, and he was with the lady he loved. Their meal finished, Liem gathered up the debris and dropped it into a nearby garbage container. Liem sat back beside Finnlea and reached for her hand. He was content to sit there and just wait for Finnlea to speak.

Finnlea watched Liem, surprised that he had not spoken. Most people would feel that they needed to fill the silence with words. Liem was like her. Silence was not something that was needed to be filled or feared.

"What do you want to know, Liem?" Finnlea leaned against his shoulder, drawing strength from him.

"Just tell me what happened." Liem looked down at her.

So Finnlea did, telling how she felt and what she had been told. The bomb had in fact no trigger. It was felt that it had been left to terrify her. The man found hiding? He was thought to be part of the group who had left the bomb. It was felt that he was to nab Finnlea when she found the bomb. Only she had not cooperated with their plans. Finnlea had not approached the house and instead called the police. That had frustrated their plans.

Liem listened carefully, knowing that she was not leaving anything out. He wondered what Paul's thoughts were on this.

"God stopped you last night, sweetheart. He didn't let you approach the house. If you had, you would have disappeared." Liem thought about what had happened.

"I know that He did. I just wish this was all over. I want to know who is stalking me."

"I get that. We've looked into your family and friends. Even at your employees." Liem's voice paused. "I know of a lady who can search for us. A friend is married to her cousin." Liem reached for his phone and sent a quick email to the lady. He tucked away his phone, knowing that he would hear back from her.

On her feet, Finnlea tugged Liem to his feet. He grabbed for the blanket and walked them back to his truck. Once behind the steering wheel, he turned to her with a question on his face.

"I didn't put down where I was working at the time the photos were taken. I need to do that."

"That may well be what you do need to do. Let me call Lorcan and have him meet us." He grinned as Finnlea snorted.

"There's no need to do that. He'll just show up." Finnlea bit at her upper lip. "Will this help?"

"It might. The more information that we can rule out the better it is. This has been going on for too many years." Liem parked in her driveway and was quickly walking her into the house. He headed or the kitchen to start a pot of coffee. Finnlea disappeared to change into more casual clothing before she headed for her office. She stood and stared down at the stack of photos and notes, her thoughts muddled.

Liem wrapped his arms around Finnlea. He was not surprised at how tense she was. He fully expected that. Lorcan and Lora had arrived and were amicably squabbling in the kitchen. The men loved their aunt deeply but weren't averse to arguing amicably with her. Lora simply laughed at them and told them that she was developing their debating skills.

Finnlea walked away from Liem, the stack of papers in errands. Dropping them onto the dining room table, she hesitated as she stared at them before she separated them into years. She then reached for a marker and began to note whether she was at school or working and if working where she had been working.

Lorcan shared a look with Liem before he began to read the new notes that she was making. Liem stood beside his brother, reading as well. He reached for a pad of paper and began to note everything. He frowned. There seemed to be no pattern to what he was reading. At least, he didn't think there was.

"Finnlea? Is there any significance to the dates?" Liem looked up at her.

Finnlea shrugged. She had wondered at that but the dates meant nothing to her.

"Not that I know of." She looked around at him. "Should they?"

"I wonder if there is a significance to them. I wondered if they were connected to any important dates to you or your family." Liem stared down at his notes. They were muddled, he felt, and he needed to sort through them. He walked away to pace the backyard, worried about his lady.

Lorcan frowned for a moment. He studied the list of employers.

"Finnlea, did you know that some of these are connected to this town?"

"They are? I had no idea. I just moved every couple of years, trying to find somewhere I could find myself feeling at home." She stared down at the last photo that she held in her hand. It showed her standing outside of her store just one month previously. "It's not making any sense." Finnlea was discouraged and disheartened. That was not her.

Liem reappeared, his eyes on his lady, He had had a reply to his email and needed to speak with Finnlea about it. He hesitated to speak, having heard what Lorcan had just asked Finnlea and her response.

Finnlea turned at that point and saw Liem watching her. She frowned at him, waiting for him to speak.

"Liem?" Finnlea approached him, his hands on her arms stopping her forward walk.

"Finnlea, I heard back from the lady we talked about. She wants to meet with you."

"I see. It has to be outside of my store hours." Finnlea pushed away from him and paced the room.

Chapter 25

The next day, the Monday, Finnlea backed away from the front door of her house and allowed Liem to enter. She felt his arm around her as a couple slightly older than herself entered behind him.

"Finnlea, this is Abe and Emma Finlay. He has a security team. Emma has a business which she uses to help find people and solve mysteries." Liem drew her back into the kitchen. "She needs to go over what we have found."

Emma grinned at Finnlea.

"Liem has put it in short form what I do." Emma reached to hug Finnlea. "Let's spend some time in prayer and then we'll discuss what you have found. You three are too close to this situation. Sometimes, fresh eyes that are not as close to the situation can sometimes help."

An hour later, Emma walked through the dining room, eying the piles of documents. She read through them with Abe taking photos of each page. The couple shared a look, knowing that Finnlea was in danger. They had had their own dangerous adventure. More importantly, Abe's sister had been stalked for years with her first husband of just a few months killed by that person.

Emma paused once more at a photo taken about three years previously. Her finger touched it.

"You were in our town. Finnlea, how long were in Riverville?"

Finnlea moved to stand beside Emma. She picked up the photo and stared at it. She could hear Liem and Abe speaking in the kitchen with the odd bit of laughter sounding from one of the men.

"Riverville? That was three years ago. I was there for a week or so just on vacation." Finnlea blinked rapidly as she realized the ramifications of what Emma had asked. She paled. "He's been tracking me on vacation as well."

"It seems that you have been stalked. What you are facing is growing more dangerous. Whoever it is has started to ramp up his attack on you. Liem is in danger as well just because he is being seen with you. That happened to Abe's sister. Rebecca and Gideon fell in love and married quickly. He was targeted because of that." Emma's face grew thoughtful. "We have a friend that I'll send your way. She has a store similar to yours. More importantly, she is a retired forensics psychologist and will do a profile for you as to who it is that is behind this. In fact, she doesn't need to meet to do that. Let me have the contact information for the investigator. She has kept up her credentials. She only does this for friends."

"But I don't know her. She can't do that."

Emma laughed even as she pulled out her phone and read the text that she had just received.

"Darcy and Doug are in town. Are you up to more company?" Emma grinned as Finnlea stared at her and just shrugged. "Just so you know, Doug is the lieutenant in charge of our emergency task force. And don't worry about a meal. They'll bring something.

And another friend with an Irish bakeshop sent you some goodies."

"They will? She did? I am going to owe so many people." Finnlea was in despair at the thought of the cost.

"We don't charge friends. We never do. It's how we are the hands and feet of God on earth."

Finnlea blinked rapidly as she tried to control her emotions. This was not what she had expected. She turned as she felt Liem beside her. She frowned at the couple who stood there, who smiled at her.

Late that night, Finnlea pulled the covers up tight to her neck. She was tired but she felt hopeful for the first time in days. She thanked God for her new friends. It helped her immensely to know that she was not alone in this. Hearing the stories that the two couples had shared had helped her get her perspective back. That had been badly needed.

The next morning, Finnlea headed for her store. It was closed for the day but she had work to do that could only be done there. Her mind drifted back to the day before and she smiled. The two couples who now considered her a friend had been a source of wisdom for her.

Finnlea unlocked the door and turned off the security system. She paused as she headed for her office. She shook her head. There was no way someone was in the store. Finnlea's steps paused once more before she spun and headed for the store room. She paused as she saw that the door was open. It had been closed when she walked out of the store on

Saturday. Finnlea crept forward almost on her tiptoes, a hand to her throat. She peered around the door and screamed. She backed away from the door, her hands clapped over her mouth. Not sure that she had seen what she thought thatch had seen, Finnlea crept forward once more. There really was a body on the floor. She turned and fled from the store. Pulling out her phone, Finnlea's hands were shaking almost too much to call for help.

Paul dropped a blanket over Finnlea's shoulders as he stopped beside her. A female officer stood beside her, watchful for anything out of the ordinary.

"Finnlea?" Paul's voice caused her to jump. She stared at him, her eyes huge. "What did you go and do?"

"I didn't do anything." Her voice wobbled as she responded to his question. "How did he get in there?"

"That we'll find out. Talk to me. Tell me what you found." Paul took his notes, his eyes studying Finnlea and then the store.

Finnlea told him, anger beginning to spark inside her. She was tired of being stalked. Now she felt that her store had been contaminated.

Paul walked away at last, heading for the back door of the store. He paused to speak with the crime scene techs working there before he walked inside, watching as the coroner completed the examination that he had commenced when he had arrived. The coroner stood and walked to where Paul stood.

"I would say that he's been dead since at least Saturday. Why here?"

"To terrify Finnlea, I have no doubt. Let me have your preliminary report when you can."

Chapter 26

Paul walked Finnlea into her store a couple of hours later. They were alone in it except for the patrol officer who closely followed them. Finnlea stared at the store room before she walked into it. She was grateful that Paul had called in cleaners to remove the evidence of the crime and subsequent investigation.

"Who was he, Paul?" Finnlea's voice was subdued.

"We don't know yet. He had no identification on him."

"I don't get it, Paul. The security system was set." Finnlea was troubled by that. "How did he get in?"

"On Saturday. We see him entering with another man from the front of the store. We see the other man leaving but not him." Paul watched with compassion as Finnlea stared at him in horror.

Finnlea was horrified at the thought.

"We didn't go in there after lunch. We didn't have any reason to." Finnlea paced away from the area, her stomach roiling at the thought.

Paul left at last, the female officer staying with Finnlea. Her attention was on Finnlea who was deeply shaken by what she had found.

At home a few hours later, Finnlea curled up on her couch. She had wrapped a blanket around herself, unable to stop shaking. Paul had called her earlier, just to ensure that she was all right. He had grinned as Finnlea had snorted at his question and then asked him how she was supposed to feel.

She was ignoring her phone. She knew that Liem had called and texted to her. Finnlea had simply sent back a text that she was okay but needed some time. She slept where she was even though her sleep was troubled and restless.

The next morning found Finnlea cautiously approaching the store, her keys in her hands. Eve watched her with a question on her face.

Finnlea stood inside the sore, unable to move forward.

"Finnlea? What is wrong?" Eve was puzzled.

"I found a body in the store room yesterday."

"What?" Eve was not sure that she had heard Finnlea correctly.

"A body, Eve." Finnlea explained what had transpired the day before.

Eve stared at her and then walked to open the store room door. She then turned back to Finnlea, a frown on her face.

"Finnlea? What do we do?"

"We move forward with what we have to do. We can't go backwards. It will be difficult. But I am confident that God is in control and that He is here with us."

Early that evening, Liem walked around Finnlea's house to the back yard, looking for his lady.

He found her sitting on the steps to the back porch. Sitting beside her, he wrapped an arm around her and dropped a kiss on her temple. Finnlea leaned into his hug. She knew that she needed to talk to him but she wasn't sure how to do that.

Liem began to pray for his lady, knowing that something had happened the day before. He would just wait for her to speak. When she didn't, he finally had to speak.

"What happened, sweetheart? I know that something did." His arm tightened around her.

Finnlea drew in a deep breath and then told him, her voice quavering as she did so. She refused to look at him. She heard him draw in a deep breath before he prayed for her once more.

"Has Paul said anything today?" He felt her head shake against him.

"No, he hasn't. The man had no identification on him."

"This is strange, Finnlea. And now you're not sure if you can keep the store there."

Finnlea scowled at him. As much as it disturbed her, she would not be chased away from her dream.

"I'm not moving the store. That's what they want." Finnlea's hand wrapped around his. "I can't. If I close the store, I won't open it again. I won't let whoever it is win. I won't let them destroy my dream. I know God is here and protecting us."

"He is, sweetheart." Liem was angry that this had happened to his lady. He wanted vengeance and knew that he had to step back from that and let God be the avenger.

"I am afraid, Liem. I am afraid for my customers. I can't close the store."

"No, you can't. We can find someone to come in as security during the time when you are there." Liem was thinking through what they could do.

"That might work. I could change the hours but that would not help all that much." Finnlea sigh. "I want this over, Liem. It's changing me and I don't like it." She was angry at that.

"I know that you are scared and angry. It's how we as humans react to circumstances. It's not wrong to feel that way. It's when we hold on to those feelings and let them warp and changes us that it becomes a problem."

"That's too true, Liem. I have seen it happen." Her voice died away.

Liem tilted his head to watch her face. She had remembered someone, he decided.

"It was someone in my past. Someone who knew my family. We weren't close to him or his family. He killed himself and his family grew bitter. They were shunned in the community." She turned to look at Liem. "How do we find about that family?"

Liem nodded. Finnlea was beginning to think deeply about her past.

"We send his name and what information that you can remember. Lorcan will want it as well." Liem was content to sit and hold his lady.

Chapter 27

Liem paced Lorcan's office late that evening. His brother was finishing off an investigation when Liem had arrived. Lorcan kept shooting glances at his brother, seeing the anger hovering just below the surface. He finally set aside the finished investigation. He rose and stretched before heading for the kitchen. He had not taken time for a meal and needed to find something to eat.

"Liem? What happened?"

"What happened? Finnlea found a body in her store room yesterday."

Lorcan's hands stopped as he reached for plates. He turned to stare at his brother.

"Did I hear you right? A body? In the store room?"

"That's right. Paul told Finnlea that the man entered her store on Saturday and didn't leave. How do I keep her safe?"

"That's a good question. I can work from there most days. Saturdays? You would be there. Only she'll feel smothered."

"She will." Liem pulled back a chair and sat. He reached automatically for the plate that Lorcan was shoving at him.

"We have to do this, Liem. Someone needs to look after her." Lorcan grinned as Liem laughed. "I know. She'll say that she can take care of herself."

"She can. I know that. It's just that I don't want her to. I want to be the one taking care of her."

"And she gets that. And she is afraid for you. She'll do what she can to protect you." Lorcan bit into his sandwich, his thoughts troubled.

Liem stared down at his own sandwich, unable to raise it to his mouth. He shoved aside the plate, reaching instead for a bottle of water. Just how they would protect Finnlea was an unknown, but he knew that he would be working on that.

Late that night, Liem paced his own office. He was disturbed at what Finnlea had explained had transpired the day before in the store. Finnlea had tried hard to downplay her fears. It had not worked out as well as she had wanted it to.

Reaching for his phone, he read the response that Abe had sent him. Abe would head his way the next evening. He was willing to meet with both Liem and Finnlea if they were agreeable. Liem breathed a sigh of relief. Surely, Abe would be able to give them advice.

Finnlea stared at Liem the next evening. She had been sorting through some store paperwork when he had shown up. He had hugged her and then said that Abe was on his way. Did she have time to meet with him?

She shoved away from him, angry that she had to set aside her plans for the evening. She didn't like that. She knew that he was trying to protect her but he was beginning to smother her.

"Why, Liem? What can he tell us?"

"He has a security team. It's his business to keep people safe. He can give us advice as to what we can do that doesn't smother you and will let you live your life." Liem walked away to answer the door, letting Abe and Doug in. "She'll fight us, guys, but we need to do this."

Finnlea turned as she heard the footsteps approaching her. She drew in a deep breath, her eyes on Liem. This is it, she decided. What would Abe have to say?

"Finnlea? How are you?" Abe's keen eyes studied her, a slight smile on his face as she studied him back.

"I have no idea how to feel," Finnlea scowled at Abe as his grin widened.

"That's fair, Finnlea." Abe moved to perch on the edge of her desk. "What can we do for you? Doug has experience with hostages. I have experience in keeping people safe."

"I understand that. I just don't see how it will work." Finnlea settled back in her chair with her arms folded.

"That is something that we can't guarantee will happen. You are still at risk and will continue to be until whoever it is has been apprehended. First, I would like to send my team member who does security systems. He'll go through your store and your homes." Abe looked around at Liem. "Liem, we need to give you some advice on how to stay safe. They have proven that they will go after you to get to Finnlea. I don't know how close you two are. It's frankly not our business at present. That may change." Abe shared a look with Doug who was nodding. "I don't want to scare you but it will become worse. Emma is deep into this and is quite concerned. She feels that she should have a preliminary report by tomorrow."

Abe and Doug went over everything that they could think of that might happen and gave what advice that they could give. All four knew that no matter how well prepared the couple might be, there was always the unknown. That unknown factor was something no one could prepare for.

Liem wrapped Finnlea into a hug, feeling her returning it. It worried him what had happened.

"You need to leave, Liem. Your day starts early." Finnlea locked up after him, heading to tidy away the debris from their snack. She then headed for her bed, exhausted and discouraged.

The next morning, Liem stared around his jobsite. He could hear the noise and voices from the other trades. He usually enjoyed his work. Today was different. Today he just wanted to be with Finnlea.

Chapter 28

Saturday found Finnlea and Eve busier than they had been before. Liem had stepped in to help, running the cash register for her. He had a ready grin and kind words for each one he served. He kept an eye on Finnlea, finding her scowling at him more than once.

Finnlea waved as Eve walked away at the end of the day. She was exhausted. This had been the busiest day that she had experienced since she opened up her store. Finnlea was grateful for Liem's assistance that day. She had watched him as he interacted with the customers when he didn't know that he was being observed.

Liem reached to wrap Finnlea in his arms with a kiss dropped on the top of her head.

"What do we do now?" Liem was content just to stand and hold her.

"I need to ring off the cash and do the deposit." Finnlea had locked the door after Eve. "Thank you for your help, Liam. I don't know that we could have done it without you." She leaned back in his arms to study his face.

"I was glad to be here. I enjoyed it." Liem watched as she walked away before he reached for the bank bag. "Let's deposit this. Then, if you will, I would like to take you out for a meal."

"Thank you, Liem. I have had a craving for a hamburger." She grinned as they walked out to his truck.

A short time later, Liem reached for Finnlea's hand before he asked a blessing on their food. They ate without much conversation, just happy to be together.

"Liem? Have you received anything?" Finnlea had not received anything more herself. Paul had been around the day before, just asking if she had anything more to give him.

"No, I haven't." Liem sighed. He was worried about his lady. "Have you heard from Emma?"

"I did. She's working on it but was pulled into an urgent investigation. She's hoping to be back on our problem by Monday." Finnlea sipped at her soft drink. "I haven't looked at it all week." She was embarrassed to admit that.

"It's okay, sweetheart. We needed to take a break from it. Aunt Lora asked if you would like to come for lunch tomorrow." Liem didn't push her. He was not willing to have her walk away from him and he felt that pushing her would do just that.

Finnlea shrugged. She had no plans for Sunday. At least, she hadn't. She nodded, exhaustion hitting hard. Liem rose and stuffed their garbage in the bin. His hand drew her to her feet.

Sunday found Finnlea tucked between Liem and Lorcan. Lora had found her before she headed for the children who she was teaching that morning. She watched the two men, knowing that they were both alert and ready to protect her. She didn't know how she felt about that. Her attention was caught by the songs from the worship team. Finnlea relaxed as she listened. God was speaking to her and working in her heart.

Lora turned from her kitchen counter as she put the finishing touches to their lunch. She smiled as she heard her nephews teasing Finnlea. She was giving back as good as the two brothers were dishing out. She was putting them in their place. Lora decided that Finnlea was exactly who Liem needed.

Liem headed for his aunt, a wide grin on his face. He was deeply worried about his lady. He wanted to hear what Lora thought. Finnlea had provided a copy of the material to her. He was confident that she had an opinion but would not give it until she was asked. It was just who she was.

Finnlea studied Lora, seeing that she sat back down with the pile of paper.

"Finnlea, I have read through all this material. I have also prayed over it. I am concerned about your safety. Liem, I am also concerned about you. Whoever it is has already tried to harm you. They will continue to go after you to get to Finnlea. How do we keep the two of you safe?"

Liem had focused his attention on Lora, hearing her concern for them underlying her words. He nodded, a hand reaching for Finnlea's. Lora had gone to the heart of the matter, he decided.

"There's no easy way to do that, Aunt Lora. We can take all the precautions that we can and still be harmed." Liem was frustrated at that.

Finnlea turned to study him. She had spent time in prayer that morning about that very fact.

"We need to remember that it is God who is in control. He knows the path that we are walking. This is where we have to trust Him, as hard as it is. He has only the best in His plans for us. If it means that we die, then it is the plan that He has for us."

Liem had kept his eyes as she spoke. He nodded. She had expressed what he too had realized. He could see Lorcan nodding as well.

"What you said?" Liem was finally able to control his emotions well enough to be able to speak. "We forget that our wishes and desires are not necessarily what He has planned for us. Thank you for reminding us. Aunt Lora? What did you discover? I know that you found something."

"I did. I realized as well that Finnlea and I were at a ladies' conference a number of years ago. I believe that we share a prayer group for that weekend."

Finnlea stared at Lora. She had not recognized Lora but had felt that she seemed familiar.

"That was in Riverville." She paled. "They took my photo there. Emma recognized the setting."

Lora was nodding. She had spoken with Emma the day before. Emma had called her, just to touch base with her. Unknown to Liem, she and Emma were friends.

"She would. She has a memory like no one else I have seen."

Chapter 29

Liem shifted on his chair to stare at his aunt. This was not what he had expected to hear. He knew that his aunt was quiet about those that she met. He would have thought that she would have commented on knowing Finnlea. He caught the look on Finnlea's face and just wrapped an arm around her. Liem could tell that she was distressed and anxious.

Not surprisingly, the four were not able to come to any conclusions that made sense. Liem watched Finnlea lock her door after him late that afternoon. He sighed to himself. It was getting harder and harder to walk away from her. She just wasn't ready yet to hear that he loved her.

Finnlea leaned against the locked door, a soft smile on her face. She could see that Liem was struggling not to tell her how he felt. He showed her in so many ways that he did indeed love her. She loved him back. Finnlea just didn't know when the right time to tell him would be, The ringing of her phone drew her from her reverie. It was her father's brother, the uncle who had taken her in when her parents had disappeared on a trip overseas and were presumed deceased. She was too young at the time to have many memories of her parents.

Setting aside her phone, Finnlea was troubled by the conversation with her uncle. She had not expected to hear that the authorities in the country where her parents had disappeared reached out to him. They were trying to find Finnlea but they would not say why. They had agreed to a conference the following day. Finnlea was not sure what to expect. She knew without a doubt that Liem would take the time to be there if she asked him to. She would need to pray that over.

The soft chime of her phone had her reaching for it. Liem had sent a text, just asking if he could spend the next afternoon with her. His work was held up by the delay with another trade. He ended his text with a number of red hearts. Finnlea's fingers flew over the keyboard just saying yes. She hesitated for a moment before she added a red heart. She shrugged as she did so. He had been open with her. She could do no less.

Liem's arm was around her the next afternoon. They had shared a meal and then spent time in prayer. Finnlea had explained to Liem what she knew about her parents. He had simply wrapped her into a hug, holding her tightly and prayed for her.

Finnlea swallowed hard when the police officer from that foreign country came on the line. She had no idea what to expect. She had called her uncle the night before, just to get his impressions. The man who had served as her father for most of her life had no answers for her. That troubled both of them.

Finnlea reacted in surprise, shock, and then horror as they listened to the information that was being provided to them. Liem's pen was scratching across the pad of paper, noting what information they were being told. Finnlea kept shooting glances at Liem, seeking reassurance from him. He continued to pray for his lady and her family.

Finnlea set her phone on the table, her movements slow ad hesitant. Her thoughts were troubled. Turning as she heard Liem's quiet voice, she was swept into a tight hug. She began to weep, the burden on her emotions just exploding within her.

All Liem could was to hold his lady. He turned her phone to study it as it chimed. It did not surprise him that her uncle was reaching out to her. Her emotions were finally spent. Finnlea took with gratitude the warm damp cloth that Liem handed her. She was embarrassed at weeping as she had done.

Liem set a mug of coffee in front of her before he sat himself, his hands reaching for hers. His thumbs rubbed at the back of her hands. He didn't speak. He was just there for her.

"Liem? Did I hear him correctly?"

"You did, sweetheart. He said that they found a couple who they believe are your parents." Liem's finger reached to flick away a wayward tear. "I was not expecting to hear that. I have asked Emma to confirm it. If it is true, Abe and his team will head there."

"They will?" Finnlea's energy level dropped rapidly. "I'm so tired." She yawned as she reached for her phone and read the text message from her uncle. "Uncle Fergus and Aunt Sara are heading this way. It's been so many years, Liem. I was about six when they headed over there. I was left with Uncle Fergus. He is so much like how I remember my father." She blinked at him.

"That's good. You need your family with you. When do they arrive?"

"Tomorrow." Finnlea sighed. "This doesn't help solve what we are involved in." She suddenly looked up in horror. "What if this is what it has been about?"

Liem was nodding. She had just gone to the heart of it. He reached for his phone, his eyes on Finnlea. She watched him, a sad, subdued look on her face.

"We need to speak with Paul. He needs to know this." His phone was back on the table as he rose to his feet and walked to the door. He stared at Paul as the detective entered. "Paul? I was just about to call you."

"You were? I'm here to talk with your lady. I was intending to track you down later." Paul's portfolio hit the table before he reached to pour himself a mug of coffee. "Finnlea?" He watched her closely as he sat near her.

Finnlea shook her head. Her emotions were too raw for her to speak. When she didn't speak, Paul shifted his gaze to Liem. Liem simply told him what Finnlea had just been told.

Shocked, Paul sat back in his chair before he reached for his pen. He quickly jotted down his notes, asking questions for clarification as he needed to. Whatever Finnlea had been told? This way not what he expected to hear.

"Finnlea? Are you okay?" Paul's question cut through the thick silence in the room just as a knife would do.

Finnlea shook her head. She had no idea how she was to feel. It had been her dream as a child to have her beloved parents come home. That dream had died away as she grew to an adult. Yet a snippet of that dream had been lain deep in her heart.

"I don't know, Paul. They still are working through that investigation. How is that related to what is happening here?"

Chapter 30

Finnlea curled up in a chair late that night. She knew that she needed to sleep but she knew that she would not be able to. Liem had been reluctant to leave her but had eventually prayed for her and left. Finnlea was deeply troubled. She didn't know how to feel about this new development. All she could do was pray.

Liem walked rapidly towards Finnlea as she stood on his front porch. She had headed for him once she had closed the store. Her thoughts and emotions were in turmoil. He wrapped her into a hug before turning them to his house.

"Go and get cleaned up, Liem. I'm content to wait here." Finnlea found her favourite chair on his porch. Just to be near him had calmed her down to some extent. Liem nodded and walked away. His lady was hurting and he didn't know how to help her other than just to be there for her, hold her, and pray for her.

Finnlea looked as Liem scooped her into his arms and then claimed her seat. She settled back against him, content to be held. She could feel his love for her from how he held her.

"Okay, sweetheart?"

Finnlea shrugged. She didn't know how to respond.

"Uncle Fergus wasn't able to make it today. And I haven't heard from the officer again. How did I know that they are telling the truth?" Finnlea felt that she had spent too much time on it that day.

"He didn't? Emma is working on it. She'll call us when she has something confirmed. In the meantime, would you like to go find something to eat?"

Finnlea shrugged. She was on her feet and headed for the stairs. Liem followed her to her home where she left her car and climbed into his truck. She stared at him for a moment, looking lost. He just had to kiss her.

Two days later, Finnlea turned from where she was setting up a new display, finding Emma beside her. Emma hugged her and then looked around the store. She walked away to look over the goods that Finnlea carried. Abe grinned at Finnlea before he hugged her as well.

Finnlea frowned at Abe, not sure why they were there.

"Abe?"

"It's okay, Finnlea. Emma has news and wanted to go over it with you in person. How soon do you close your shop?"

"About now. I've done what I need to for the day." Finnlea followed them out of the store, locking it behind them. "Liem will be around my place shortly." She bit at her lip. She had been putting off shopping for groceries and knew that she didn't have enough to feed them all.

"Don't worry about feeding us, Finnlea. We invited ourselves. That means that we provide the meal." Emma shivered as she looked around. "Let's get you home."

Finnlea nodded, knowing that Emma was picking up on whatever had been troubling her during the day. Abe followed her home, his eyes narrowing as he watched the car following them. He nodded. Finnlea was being followed. He knew from speaking with Liem that either he or Lorcan was searching her car every morning. Liem had laughed as he described the scowl that she bestowed on them when they did that search.

Finnlea stood on her front lawn, frowning at the cars parked in front of her house. Her purse dropped to the ground as she flew across the lawn to be wrapped in the lady's arms before the man claimed her. The man stood back at last before he turned her to face her home.

"You need to introduce us to your friends." Her uncle nudged her forward.

Finnlea introduced her aunt and uncle to the group that had gathered near her driveway. Liem, Lorcan, and Lora had appeared. Abe moved them into her home, his eyes on the car once more that had parked across the street from Finnlea's house. He shared a look with Lorcan who decided to return to his car. He managed to snag a photo of the car and forwarded it to Paul.

Lora and Sara headed for the kitchen, taking the bags of food from Emma. Their conversation was quiet as they listened to the voices from the others. They shared a look as they heard Finnlea's voice raised at one point and then stared at her as she ran by them. Liem was on her heels, intent on protecting his lady.

Abe stood at the back door, watching the two before he was running after them and shoving them back into the house. His keen eyes had caught movement at the back of the yard.

Finnlea spun to take Abe on, her mouth opening and closing. He simply stared back at her. She was not the first lady who tried to take him on and lost. He had been tried by some of the best and still kept them alive.

Finnlea disappeared from the kitchen. Abe walked over to watch her as she headed for what he assumed was her bedroom, the door closing quietly behind her. Emma tapped at the door and entered, simply sitting beside Finnlea and praying for her.

Finnlea swiped at her face. She did not cry but felt as if that was all she was doing later. She blinked to clear her eyes.

"How did you do it, Emma?" Finnlea drew in a deep breath. "There is just so much happening lately. I am just so confused."

"And God knows how you feel. I can't tell you how many times at the beginning that I yelled at God, got angry, walked away from Him, screamed, cried, repented, and did it all over again. Abe was the same. God understands, Finnlea. He does not want us to hide from Him. He is our Abba father. Murphy, Abe's business partner and a good friend, has a saying. He looks at it this way: God has a plan and purpose for us that we don't understand or see. And that has proven so true."

Finnlea nodded slowly. Emma was correct. God didn't want His children to hide their emotions. He had provided a Comforter for them, after all.

Chapter 31

Fergus watched his niece closely that evening. He was worried about her, that went without saying. Sara had approached her after everyone else had left but Finnlea had not opened up to her as she had done in years past. That told him how deeply Finnlea was burying what was bothering her. And she would not talk to them. Fergus smiled to himself as he remembered the face-off between Liem and Finnlea that had occurred as the younger man was leaving. Neither one backed down from the other. Sara had just walked up to them and told them off before walking away. Fergus had caught the motion with his hand that Liem had made as he tried to cover his grin. That had caused Finnlea to glare even more at him. Liem had simply swept her into a hug and then walked out of the door with her.

Liem studied his lady before he left. She was deeply troubled and he could not make it better for her. Only God could do that, he knew.

"I'm praying for you, sweetheart. Will you be okay tonight?" He tightened his hug on her, reluctant to let her go.

Finnlea shrugged.

"I have no idea. I worry about my family here. And I don't know what to think of what Emma has provided."

"She has her doubts about that couple. Abe told me that his team is flying over there at the request of the federal authorities. They leave in the morning." Finnlea nodded soberly.

"That's what he said. I have something else to worry about now." Finnlea shoved at Liem as she felt his body shaking. "This isn't funny, buster."

"No, it's not. Your comment was just you." Liem reached to kiss his lady before he reluctantly walked from her. It was getting harder and harder to do that.

Finnlea watched him drive away, her arms wrapped around herself. She knew that Fergus and Sara were waiting to talk with her. She just wasn't ready to have that conversation. She had walked into the house, avoiding Fergus and Sara, and headed for her office. She needed to do some office work that she had not been able to get.

A mug of coffee landed on the desk beside her as Fergus headed to a scat on the other side of the desk. He watched her as she worked away, her hands flying over the papers. Fergus waited patiently for Finnlea to look up.

Finnlea sat back as she eyed her uncle. He had never pushed her. Instead, Fergus had simply let her know that he was there when she wanted to talk. He also let her know that he was praying for her.

"Uncle Fergus? What do you think about all of this?" Finnlea knew her uncle would have been thinking through everything.

Fergus nodded, watching as Sara entered and set a tray down on the table near the couch. Finnlea was on her feet to reach to hug her aunt.

"Finnlea, love, we don't know if these people are your parents. We have to wait to find that out. My feeling is that they are not. I know that you hope that they are. It would be difficult for you after all these years. You were raised differently from how they would have raised you."

Finnlea nodded, sadness on her face. They had had this conversation at different times over the years.

"I just wonder if it is related to what we are going through. I know that I am being watched and followed all the time. This would throw off my attention to what is happening here and make me vulnerable."

Fergus was nodding. Finnlea had gone right to the heart of her adventure.

"That is our thinking, Finnlea. This is distracting you from being careful. That I know that you are trying to do. Life gets in the way." Fergus prayed for his niece.

"That's what's happening, Uncle Fergus. I am trying hard. It's worrying at the store as so many strangers are there."

Sara and Fergus share a look. They had heard the tone in Finnlea's voice as she spoke of Liem. She would not be coming back to her hometown.

"Finnlea, we will not pry into your feelings for Liem. We can see that he cares deeply for you. If he is

God's chosen mate for you, then we welcome him into our family. We know that you won't move back to our town. We must confess that we have missed you deeply. That being said, now that we are retired, we would like to know your feelings about us moving here."

Finnlea gaped at her aunt, her mouth open, before she was hugging her. Fergus wrapped his ladies in his arms. That Finnlea was happy about that decision was obvious.

"Your house?" Finnlea at back, happiness on her face knowing that her family was moving to her town.

"It's been sold. The movers have already packed everything and put it in storage. We just need to find house here." Fergus grinned at her.

Finnlea walked her store the next day. Her cmotions were in a turmoil. She was happy that Fergus and Sara would be here. She turned as she heard footsteps approaching her. She stared at the man who stood there, a grin on his face.

"I'm sorry. Do I know you?"

"No, you don't. I'm Richard, a friend of Abe's. Abe asked if my team could move in just for today. Let me explain. I'm from Elmton and have a security team as well. Abe was called out on a rush protection detail but had heard that an attempt would be made on you today. He wanted someone with you. He reached out to you this morning."

Finnlea paled as she reached for her phone. Richard was correct. Abe had reached out but she had not heard the chimes for the messages. She had muted her phone the night before and had forgotten to unmute it.

Chapter 32

Finnlea paced away from Richard, unsettled that Abe had felt the need to call in a friend. She turned back to study Richard, observing the two men and two ladies who stood near him. She strode back to stand in front of him, frowning at him.

"I can't have all of you in here. And Liem needs protection as well."

"We understand that, Finnlea. I will leave Silver and Naomi with you. Stephen and Timothy will be with Liem. That works for today during the day. I will float between the two sites." Richard's face was grim.

Finnlea shrugged. It looked as if the decisions had been taken out of her hands. She walked towards the back of the store where she had new stock waiting for her.

Liem stood beside his truck, watching Stephen and Timothy as they searched his truck. He stared at the devices that they had removed from his truck.

"All those?" Liem was shocked.

"All these." Timothy's voice was stern.

"What about Finnlea's vehicle?" Liem was ready to race to her store and protect her.

"Richard was taking care of it." Stephen pointed at Liem's truck. "Head for your home, Liem. We need to search there. The ladies will search her store and then they'll search around her home."

"I see." Liem drove towards his home, Stephen seated in the cab beside him. "How do we do this, Stephen? Abe has given lots of advice. Some we can do but there are some that just aren't feasible." He rubbed at the back of his neck.

"We get that, Liem. Abe had a conference call last night with us. We know what he advised. It's what Richard would have advised. Let us search your place as you get cleaned up and then we'll get you to your lady."

Liem rushed to change from his work clothes and then found the two men waiting for him. He didn't like the look on their faces. He drove towards Finnlea, growing increasingly worried about his lady. He watched as Timothy and Stephen strode towards Richard. Liem walked towards the house and Finnlea. She in turn moved into his hug before the two ladies shoved them into the house. The door was closed and locked. Liem watched through the door window as first Paul and then a crime scene team appeared.

Finnlea stood behind him, a hand resting on his back. She was distressed at the sight. She had no idea what had been found but it could not be good.

Silver and Naomi searched inside of the house, not finding anything. That was a relief for them at the moment. There was no telling if that would change one point.

Paul and Richard both walked towards the house about an hour later. Finnlea by that time had found her seat behind her computer. Liem sat nearby, answering emails for his work. They both looked up as Paul dropped into a chair facing the two of them.

Finnlea sighed. This would not be good news. She prayed for protection and an answer for what they were going through.

"Paul? What did you find?"

"Cameras around your house, Finnlea. They are watching you very carefully. And I want to know why." Paul sounded angry. They had evidence in the case but nothing that explained it or tied it together.

"Of course you would. It's what you always find, isn't it? Now, what do we do to bring whoever it is out into the open? I want this over." Finnlea was angry.

"It is, Finnlea. Unfortunately, the people who are doing this are being very careful. They aren't leaving any evidence about themselves." Paul frowned at Finnlea. "What are you planning?"

"Me? I'm planning on finding them." Finnlea glared at him. "What do you expect me to do?"

"Let us find them?" Paul was not hopeful that she would do just that.

"You have been trying, Paul, but you haven't found them." Finnlea was on her feet and headed for the printer. As she walked back past him, she dropped the pile of papers into his hands. Paul stared at her and then the papers.

"What is this?" Paul glanced through the papers.

"Plans to catch whoever it is. I am not prepared to sit back any more."

Paul share a look with Liem who seemed just as determined as Finnlea was to go on the offensive. He shook his head. He could not stop them, he knew, but he was afraid that they were headed into something that they were not prepared to face. Paul began to read, impress with their plans. He suspected that Abe had been involved in their plans.

"When do you plan on implementing these?" Paul held up the papers.

"As soon as we can." Finnlea scowled at Liem who was simply watching her. "We want this over with and now."

"I see. And will you let us work with you?"

Paul's question was not what Finnlea had expected. She shared a long look with Liem, waiting for Liem to speak.

Liem nodded, knowing that they needed Paul's help.

"We welcome your assistance, Paul. But we are not sitting back any more. It's taking too much from us." Liem scrubbed at his face with his hands.

"We know that it is. We regret that we have not been able to solve it." Paul read through the papers once more, noting how precise and complete the plans were.

Chapter 33

That Saturday, Liem walked the downtown area of his town. He was putting himself out there, just as they had planned. He would head for Finnlea shortly. For now, he was searching for anyone who was tracking him or wanting to harm him.

Giving up for the day, Liem headed for his truck and then for Finnlea. He sat for the longest time just watching the store and the number of customers who entered and exited it. He smiled at the happy looks on their faces. He locked his truck as he headed that way, smiling at the little girl who excitedly chattered about the rag doll that she was clutching in her arms.

Finnlea leaned back against Liem as he wrapped an arm around her. He whispered a prayer in her ear and then dropped a kiss on her cheek.

"Having a good day, sweetheart?" Item grinned at her nod. "That's good. I walked the down town as we planned."

"Did you?" Finnlea turned her head to face him. "So, it's starting."

"It is." Liem's arm tightened on her before he moved away to crouch down by a little boy who was gently touching a wooden train.

Finnlea smiled to herself before she turned back to her customers. Eve watched the couple before she smiled.

Paul was waiting for the couple as they walked towards Liem's truck. He grinned at Finnlea as she stared at him.

"Liem. Finnlea. I'm off duty." He held up a bag. "Liem, we haven't grilled for a while."

"No, we haven't. That sounds good. We'll follow you to your place."

Finnlea studied the traffic around them. It was heavier than normal.

"There's a lot of traffic tonight." Finnlea watched Liem's face as it t tightened. "Liem?"

"There is. I can't keep close to Paul. Let him know." Liem shot her a look that showed how worried he was.

Finnlea reached for her phone before she screamed. Liem slammed on the brakes before his head was twisting as he searched for a way out of the box that three vehicles had trapped him in. He spun the truck steering wheel and felt the tires climbing the curb onto the paved parking lot. He drove rapidly or as rapidly as he could and out of the lot.

Finnlea kept watch for the vehicles as Liem drove a zigzag path to Paul's house. He lifted Finnlea over the console and set her on her feet. He snatched her hand and pulled her towards the house. Paul pointed to the door and heard it shut. He ran towards Liem's truck and searched it. There was nothing on it. Once back inside his home, Paul found Finnlea clinging to Liem. He didn't like the look of anger on his friend's face.

"Liem? Talk to me. What happened? And don't tell me that nothing did."

"We were boxed in near Joe's grocery store. I was able to climb the curb and drive away. They got inbetween us." Liem was trying to tamp down his anger. All he could do was thank God that He had helped them get away.

"You were? I wondered why you weren't right behind me. Did you recognize anyone?"

"No. I couldn't see because of the tint on the windows. And I didn't recognize the trucks." Liem watched as Finnlea shoved away from him and disappeared into the kitchen. Both men could hear the rustling of plastic and then the opening and closing of cupboards. "Let's eat, Paul. Then, we need to spend some time in prayer. We need that."

"That you do." Pau walked into the kitchen to find Finnlea watching him. "I'll have the grill ready in a moment for the chicken."

Finnlea nodded, having already reached that conclusion. She turned back to the potatoes that she was stuffing into the microwave to partially cook before they would land on the grill as well. Paul's hand landed briefly on her shoulder before he headed for the back door.

Liem's heart broke for his lady. He so wanted this over for her and it didn't seem to be happening. He dropped a kiss on her cheek before reaching for bottles of water from the fridge. Finnlea worked away on a salad, listening to the men's quiet conversation that filled the kitchen. She was grateful that Liem had been able to remove them from the situation but it still pulled her.

An hour later, the remnants of the meal were cleaned away. The sounds of nature echoed in their ears as the men sat back down in their seats, hot beverages now in front of them. Liem reached for Finnlea's hand as their heads bowed. Silence followed for a few moments as they all struggled to release what had happened and as they prepared to seek God's presence.

Paul look-up hen they had finished their time of prayer. He reached for the pad paper and pen that he headset beside him. He was ready to find out all that he could from the couple. Paul wasn't sure if they would be able to provide much information.

Finnlea pointed at his phone as she set her on the table.

"Check your messages. I was able to snap photos of the vehicles. Maybe you can use them." She felt Liem's hand tighten on hers.

Paul shot her a surprised look before he reached for his phone. He scrolled through the photos before he sent them on to the crime lab.

"These will help. Good work on your part, Finnlea. I wish that I could say that this would end it but it won't."

"We know that it won't. We will continue with our plans." Liem bit at his lower lip, his eyes on Finnlea.

"I know that you will. Just be aware that it is going to escalate."

"We know that as well. We will take the steps that we need to take." Liem watch as Finnlea rose and then returned with the coffeepot. "We want this over."

"And it will be. We pray that neither one of you is harmed. We just can't predict what will happen."

"No one can but God. We are in His hands." Finnlea blinked back tears, fear for Liem and their families uppermost in her thoughts.

Chapter 34

Tuesday night found Liem at loose ends. Finnlea was at a meeting that would take the whole evening. He stood for a moment in his back yard before he sighed. Liem walked the perimeter of the yard, lost in thought.

The men moving quietly across the freshly-cut grass towards Liem kept their eyes on him. Hearing a whisper of sound, Liem began to turn that way but hadn't a chance to make it all the way around before he was tackled to the ground. Fists hammered him and left him bloodied and bruised before the men were on their feet and running away.

At last, Liem sat up, his arm wrapping around his abdomen. He stared at the white envelope that lay in front of him. Groaning, he leaned forward to reach for it before he was struggling to his feet and then heading with slow steps towards his home. Liem locked the door behind him. He paused for a moment, his eyes closing against the pain. He dropped the envelope to the table before he shuffled down the hall to his bedroom. His thought was that a hot shower might help. He winced at the stinging from the water hitting his body. Dressed once more, Liem headed back to the kitchen.

Liem stared at the envelope as he reached for a bottle of water and opened it. His eyes didn't move from it as he took a deep drink of the water. He frowned. He hadn't heard the men approaching him and he should have.

Reaching for the envelope, Liem hesitated before he pulled open the flap. He stared at the folded paper that was inside. Liem pulled out the paper, fear for himself and his lady wafting through him. He unfolded it and then lifted his eyes to stare at the ceiling. His prayer was for protection and understanding.

Liem stared down at the paper, not quite focused on the paper. The paper shook with the intensity of his fear before he laid it on the tabletop. He read the words, fear rising within him once more.

You are warned. We will be back. You and your lady will pay.

Frowning, Liem could not understand what the note meant. Why would they pay? And who was behind it all? He wanted to find that person and ask them that very question.

He sighed to himself before he just walked away from the kitchen, turning off the lights and heading for his rest. His body protested as he lay down and he was well aware that the next day would be even worse.

Lorcan stared at his brother the next afternoon. He had tracked Liem down as he finished work for the day. He frowned at the bruising that he could see on Liem's face.

"Liem? You're not moving very quickly. And your face is bruised." Lorcan's hand on his brother's arm stopped him in his tracks.

"I know. I took a beating last night. And yes, I did talk to Paul this morning." Liem's eyes closed for a moment against the discomfort that he was feeling. "Out of the way, Lorcan. I need to head home for a hot shower. Finnlea will be at my place once the store closes."

Lorcan watched his brother drive away before he headed for Finnlea's store. He sat in his truck, watching the foot and vehicle traffic around it. He frowned. There had to be a clue somewhere. Only none of them seemed able to find it. That was frustrating.

Finnlea stared at Liem a short time later before she moved into his arms and wrapped her arms around him. She was shocked at the sight of his face. Finnlea felt his wince as she hugged him. Trying to step back from him, Liem's arms prevented her from doing that.

"We'll talk, Finnlea. We'll talk. I'm okay for the most part. I hear Lorcan in the kitchen."

"He is. He was muttering something about a meal. I don't know that I feel like eating much."

"No, I don't either." Liem kissed her before he reached to draw her into his office. He turned to her. "I love you, Finnlea. You're the one that I want to spend the rest of my life with. Will you marry me and soon?" He reached for her left hand, a beautiful blue diamond slipping on her finger.

Finnlea blinked back tears. Liem was her knight, she knew. She could only nod before he claimed her for a kiss.

"I love you too, Liem." Her head rested against his shoulder. "But you said soon?"

"I did. I would like to marry you tomorrow but take what time you need. I won't rush you."

Finnlea was grateful for that. She stared at her ring, knowing that Liem would have prayed it through before asking her. She had been doing the same.

Lorcan stood in the hallway for a moment, watching his brother. He sighed. Liem really had to do that, didn't he? This would make this even worse for the couple. Lorcan walked into the office to hug both of them before he stood back.

"I have a meal ready for us. I'm not sure that any of us feel much like eating."

"Not likely but we need to." Liem walked out of the office, following Finnlea as she headed for the kitchen. He paused as Lorcan's hand rested on his shoulder.

"You're sure, Liem?" At Liem's nod, he sighed to himself. "It's going to be much harder on you, you do know that? A friend is one thing to worry about. This? This will make the worry that much greater."

"I know, Lorcan. I do know that. I just want what time we have with one another. It might be fifty years. It might be fifty minutes. Only God knows the length of our days."

"That is true. I'm happy for you, Liem. You and she make a great couple." Lorcan walked away for a moment, struggling to control his emotions.

Finnlea watched Lorcan over the rest of the evening before she rose to leave. She hugged him, knowing that she had gained not only a husband-to-be but a brother as well. She had always wanted a brother.

Abe turned as Emma approached him, a shuttered look on her face. It was not good news, he decided, as he swept her into a hug and then took the papers from her. He read them over before he nodded. Emma had confirmed what they had suspected. They needed to head for Finnlea but couldn't until the weekend. Work commitments prevented that.

Chapter 35

Saturday night found Finnlea staring at her aunt and uncle. This was the first time that she had seen them since becoming engaged. They were delighted with the engagement, knowing that Liem was just the man that Finnlea needed in her life.

"When is the wedding?" Sara shared a look with Fergus. "I kept your mother's wedding dress and have it with us. I thought this would be happening."

"You kept it? All these years?" Finnlea blinked back her tears. "It will be like having Mom and Dad there."

"It will. We kept as much for you as we could. Most of it you have. I didn't tell you about the dress just because I wanted to wait until you found the knight that God had planned for you."

Finnlea hugged her aunt and then found herself wrapped in Fergus' arms. His prayer caused her to weep even more. She was turned and then found herself wrapped in Liem's arms. He shared a look with Fergus before he moved Finnlea to another room and just continued to hold his lady.

Abe and Emma stood just inside the front door, staring at Sara for a moment. They felt as if they had walked into a maelstrom without knowing it.

"It's okay, Emma." Sara pointed to the kitchen. "Come on into the kitchen. Liem and Finnlea are dealing with something that brings them happiness."

Emma smiled. She had a good idea of what had happened.

"When's the wedding?" She grinned at Sara.

"Soon, I suspect. Finnlea is very emotional right now. I have her mother's wedding dress and just told her that."

"I see." Emma shared a look with Abe. "We do need to speak with her tonight. That's why we're here."

Finnlea had approached as she heard Emma speaking. Liem's arm tightened around her.

"We'll eat, sweetheart, and spend time in prayer. Then, we'll listen to what they have to tell us. Somehow, I suspect that what we were told was not the truth."

"I've come to that conclusion. It would be too strange for Mom and Dad to appear after all these years. I've researched that country. There is no way that something like that would happen there." Finnlea moved away from Liem to greet Emma.

Abe studied the couple over the meal and then bent his head to pray for them. He was very worried about them. The news that they had to share was what Emma had expected to find. Abe was just not sure how they would take the news.

Liem raised his head, his hand tightening on Finnlea's hand. He watched Abe and then Emma, finding them not showing any emotion or hint as to what they were thinking.

"Abe? You two are here for a reason." Finnlea stared between the two.

"We are. First, let us congratulate you two. You're taking a big step. And you do realize that this step also means that you become bigger targets?"

"We do." Liem sighed. "It's not how we want to start a married life together but it is what it is. God is leading us in this. Now, what do you have to tell us?"

Emma was on her feet and returned to the table where she sat quietly for a moment. Her eyes were on Finnlea, knowing that the news would be what Finnlea was expecting. Emma had kept in touch with Finnlea over the days.

"Finnlea. I have been in touch with the authorities in that country. We have been going back and forth for a few days now. I'm sorry to tell you that this couple is not your parents. They have admitted to being paid to pretend to be. The authorities in that country are continuing to hunt for your parents but believe that they are deceased as had been reported to your uncle."

Finnlea nodded soberly. It was the conclusion that she had come to. Her parents would not have willingly stayed away from her, that much she understood.

"It's okay, Emma. It's what I had come to expect. Mom and Dad would not have stayed away if they had been alive. And that many years? It would be difficult to understand that they were kept away from us unless they were dead or in prison."

"We have searched that as well, Finnlea. They are not imprisoned in that country or any country near it." Emma's face held the sympathy that she felt. "I'm sorry. I wish that I had other news for you."

Finnlea shrugged. She had already made her peace with the news, knowing that there would likely be no way that these people were her parents. Liem and she had prayed it through as well as talked it through. She stared at Fergus, seeing his emotions just below the surface.

"I'm sorry, Uncle Fergus. I wish that it had been Mom and Dad."

Fergus smiled at her through his tears. He had prayed that somehow it had been his brother and his wife.

"It is what it is, Finnlea. God knows where they are. We have come to terms that we will never see them again on earth." He was on his feet to reach and hug his niece. Finnlea clung to him for a moment before Fergus was back in his chair. "Now what, Emma? How does this impact what is going on here?"

"The photos." Liem shared a look with Abe who was nodding. "They were a set up to this. Whoever is behind this has been planning this since Finnlea's parents disappeared. That makes me think that they are involved in it. The photos would have been used to help the people fool Finnlea. Somehow, someone has realized this and is trying to help Finnlea find the ones responsible."

"That is what we suspect, Liem." Emma reached for another folder. "This is what I have discovered so far. Some of my staff are working on it now exclusively. We will solve this, Finnlea. That is our promise. God is protecting you from whatever this involves."

"I have felt that over the years, Emma. In some situations, God seemed to stop me." Finnlea paled. "Those times? I need to document them, don't I?"

Abe nodded. Emma and he had spoken about those situations, wondering if Finnlea would remember any of them. He watched as Finnlea reached for a pen and pad of paper and began to scribble frantically. He could tell that she had blocked out the conversation going on around.

Shoving the pad of paper across the table towards Emma, Finnlea leaned back against Liem, feeling spent. Emma was on her feet, heading for the office to make copies of what Finnlea had written. She would work on it and knew that Finnlea and Liem would do the same. Her phone was in her hand as she sent a copy to Paul with her findings and thoughts.

Chapter 36

Finnlea stared at the well-dressed woman who stood in her way in the local grocery store. She turned and walked away, leaving the store. She could hear the tap of high-heel shoes behind her. Finnlea entered the store next door, waved at the clerk, and then headed for the employees only door. She was through it and around to her car, driving away before the woman had emerged from the store.

Pulling to the side of the street, Finnlea buried her head in her hands. This just didn't happen, she thought. A woman had not just approached her like that. Finnlea frowned and then sighed. She knew who the woman was and that frightened her. She had heard rumours about her for months now. Her phone was out as she sent a text off to Paul. He could deal with her. Finnlea drove away and headed for another grocery store. She needed to shop and shop that night.

Liem rang the doorbell at Finnlea's house a short while later before he pounded at the door. She should be there, he thought. She had spoken with him not that long ago, telling him that she was shopping and would be home by the time that he arrived. Only, she wasn't. And that worried him too much for him not to act.

Running around the house, he searched for any sign of her and then tried the back door. It was locked as well. His phone was out as he frantically called her with no answer. Her phone went right to voice mail.

That was not like her, he knew. She was good at picking up his calls.

Paul walked towards Liem, watching as the other man paced the sidewalk in front of the home. This was not what he had wanted to hear. He was still disturbed by the name that Finnlea had sent him.

"Liem? Any sign of her?"

Paul's voice stopped Liem in his tracks. He stared at his friend, the detective, before he shook his head.

"No. She hasn't gotten home yet. Her phone is going directly to voice mail." Liem was becoming more and more agitated, totally unlike him.

"She had an incident at Joe's. Some woman approached her." Paul said the name, bringing Liem's shocked eyes to his face.

"Her? How is she involved?"

"That's what we'll be asking her. Someone is heading to bring her in for questioning. Given that, Finnlea likely headed for another store. I have a patrol officer heading that way to search for her." Paul was praying that Finnlea had just not heard her phone and that was the reason that she hadn't answered.

"I see. That makes sense. But it doesn't explain why that woman would approach her. I don't know that they are familiar with one another."

"That woman is well known in town. She hides from the authorities though. There have been rumours for years about her. We just haven't been able to prove anything."

"No, you haven't been able to." Liem paced once more, watching the traffic on the road. His steps paused as he saw a car approaching and turning into the driveway. He ran towards the car, sweeping Finnlea into his arms as she stepped from the car.

Finnlea clung to him, sobs wracking her body. Her normal feisty demeanour was being hidden in the midst of her trouble. She hated that.

"You're okay, sweetheart?" Liem leaned back to look down at her.

Finnlea nodded, her eyes on Paul. What was he doing here?

"I am. Why is Paul here?"

"I panicked and asked him to come. Let's get you inside." Liem popped open the truck and gathered up the bags of groceries. "Inside, sweetheart. We'll talk about that incident."

"We will." She stomped past Paul without a word and headed for the house. She then headed for her bedroom and reached for her comfort clothes. She blinked back tears of fear and then dropped to sit on the bed. Finnlea began to pray, needing that comfort and peace that came from God.

Paul helped Liem put away the groceries before he stood and stared out of the back door window. He was puzzled as to what had happened earlier that day to Finnlea.

Liem waited patiently in the hall for Finnlea, leaning against a wall. His eyes were on the floor as he thought through what was going on. He looked up as Finnlea approached him, simply wrapping her into his arms.

"I can't do this, Finnlea. I can't be apart from you. Marry me this week?" Liem's voice was low and broken.

Finnlea hugged him harder and nodded against him. They didn't need to make many plans. The wedding would be small, that they had agreed on.

Paul turned as he heard Finnlea entering the room. He assessed her, seeing the worry that she was trying hard to hide.

"Finnlea? Talk to me. Tell me what happened this afternoon." Paul waited patiently for her to speak.

"What happened? I went to do my shopping and she was there in front of me. I left the store and she followed me. I had to duck through a store next door and then drive across town to another store. Isn't that enough?" Finnlea's voice had risen in her anger.

Liem rubbed at his upper lip, not wanting Finnlea to know that he was hiding a grin. It didn't work. Finnlea glared at him but he could see the amusement in her eyes. Paul studied the two, not sure what to do.

"Finnlea? Have you met this woman before?" Paul finally broke through the silence with his question.

"No, I haven't. Not that I am aware of." Finnlea turned to him, a frown on her face as she thought through his question. "Should I have?"

"Not that I am aware of." Paul sighed. "She has always been someone that has been on our radar."

"I see. And she just had to choose me, didn't she?" Finnlea frowned even more. "I have no idea who she is."

Chapter 37

On that Saturday, Finnlea stared at herself in her full-length mirror. Her mother's wedding dress fit her almost perfectly. She blinked back tears, knowing that her parents could not be there as much as she wished and prayed for that. The consensus was that they were dead and their place of death would remain unknown. Liem had hugged her earlier that day as he handed her the roses that he had bought for her to carry.

Fergus stood and watched as his niece approached him. She is so like his brother's wife, he thought. His brother and his wife would be so proud of the lady in front of him.

"All set, love?" Fergus hugged her carefully, not wanting to disturb the dress or flowers. His finger flicked a wayward tear from her cheek.

"I think so." Finnlea looked up at him. "I just wish it was different."

"So do we. Flynn would have approved of your fellow. He would also be proud of the lady that you are today. So would Leah. Sara and I are grateful to have been able to step in and raise you." Fergus turned her towards the back door. "Let's get you to your fellow, love."

Late that afternoon, Finnlea turned from where she had been unpacking some of her belongings in the office at Liem's. They had decided to live in Liem's home and let Fergus and Sara have Finnlea's house. They had yet to tell them that.

"Finnlea?" Liem had come to find her, reaching to hug her and then steal some kisses from his bride.

"Liem?" Finnlea leaned back to look up at him. "You were looking for me?"

"I was. I want to take you out for dinner. If you are willing, that is."

Finnlea shrugged, fear suddenly rising within her.

"I think not, Liem. I'm scared tonight and don't want to leave home. Do you understand?"

"I do. I feel the same way. We have enough from the meal that we had earlier for a meal." Liem wrapped his arm around her once more and headed them for the kitchen.

Neither one of them heard the noise outside of their home that night that would spell danger for them in the morning. The men worked rapidly in the dark, confident in their movements in the dark night. Even the moon and stars seemed to be in cahoots with them, hiding behind the heavy dark clouds.

Finnlea was on her feet early in the morning, heading for the office. Something was puzzling her about the woman and she wanted to do some research. Lorcan had simply stated that he had sent some information to her but she was under strict orders not to look at it on her wedding day. Well, she decided, her wedding day was yesterday. That meant that she could read it this morning.

Reading through the information, Finnlea was disturbed at what she was reading. She printed off copies of what Lorcan had sent before she grabbed a highlighter and headed for the kitchen. She dropped the papers on the table, squinting at the clock, and setting the coffee before she reached for food for their breakfast. Liem hesitated in the kitchen doorway, smiling as he watched Finnlea working away before he had her in his arms.

Finnlea handed him a copy of the papers when they had cleaned up after their meal and then spent time in prayer. She was grateful that God had provided a groom for her who was a praying man. That was how she had been raised, to spend time with God about anything and everything.

"What's this?" Liem glanced through it, a frown on his face.

"Lorcan did this. He provided it for me and told me that I had to wait to read it. It's about that woman." Finnlea glanced at the clock. "We have some time before we need to head to church."

"Church. Are you ready to go in as my bride?" Liem grinned at her before he claimed a kiss.

"I am. Are you prepared to go in as my groom?" Finnlea grinned at him before she poked at the papers that he held. "How did he find all this?"

"By researching. He hears a lot from the town because of his work. He's known to be willing to talk to anyone and will keep their confidence. The only time he doesn't is if there is a crime involved. Even then, he doesn't give away his source."

"I can see that." Finnlea frowned. "I still don't understand why me."

"I sent the name on to Emma to see what she or her staff can find out. She was out of town with Abe and their son but would look into it this week when they're back." Liem rose as he glanced at the clock. "We need to leave soon, sweetheart."

"I know." Finnlea was on her feet, tidying up the papers and heading to the office with them. She hated to leave a messy house when she walked out of the door.

Liem headed for the front door and stopped as if he had walked into a brick wall. There was just no way that he could approach it. The same thing happened as he approached the back door. Finnlea stared at him in confusion.

"Liem? What are you doing?" Finnlea moved to walk by him to find herself wrapped into Liem's arms. "Liem? We need to go out one of the doors."

"We can't. God won't let me." Liem's head was moving quickly before he pulled her towards the bedroom and the window. He raised the window rapidly and shoved out the screen. He was out of the window and reaching for Finnlea before he had her hand in his and was running around the house and down the street. Finnlea's feet were moving as rapidly as she could, confused as to what Liem was doing.

"Liem? Stop! I need to know what happened!" Finnlea tugged him to a stop.

"There is something around the house, sweetheart. God wouldn't let me open the doors." Liem stared back at their home, uncertainty on his face. His phone was out as he called for help.

The responding officer walked towards where Liem and Finnlea stood, a stern look on his face.

"Liem? Finnlea? Explain to me again what happened." He watched Paul as he stood nearby, listening to the conversation.

Liem once more went through what had happened. He frowned at the officer as that man nodded.

"It's a good thing that you didn't try and go out the front door. Someone had jerry-rigged a wire from the light socket to the metal handle. If you had touched the handle, you would have been electrocuted." His voice was stern. "Chances are you would not have survived."

Liem stared at the officer and then at Finnlea. Her face was white, shock showing on it. He knew that his face was likely the very same.

Chapter 38

Paul walked away at that point, heading for the crime scene techs who were working away around the house. He had not expected to hear this and it really disturbed him. He thanked God that Liem had had the presence of mind to listen and not try to exit through a door.

"What do you have?" Paul stood back from the area.

"Whoever this is meant business, Paul." The tech stood and walked back towards him. She handed him an evidence bag. "They did this in the dark, I would suspect. They had to be good to do that with just a low light."

"That they would be. Anything else that you can tell me right now?"

"Not really. They didn't go for the windows, just the doors. That tells me that they thought Liem or Finnlea would not leave through a window. Although it would have been more difficult in the dark to rig up wiring on the windows without being heard."

"That it would. Let me know what else you find when you can."

Paul walked back towards the newlywed couple, finding them watching him closely. He had no answers for them that would satisfy them.

"Paul?" Liem's voice held the question that he would not ask.

"They were good, Liem, whoever they were. They didn't tamper with the windows. They fully expected you to touch the door." Paul's face was grim as he spoke. It had gone far enough, he decided.

"That is what we thought. We took a chance, I know, on going through the window." Liem was frustrated. This had to end and end now.

Finnlea was frustrated as well. This was going on for far too long. They were wearing out under it all. She paused in her thoughts.

"Paul? None of this has made any sense. Why me? Why my store? No threat has ever really been identified. And there should be."

"It should have been. I agree with you on that. And as to why you? We are starting to get hints as to why but not enough that we can really understand the reason." Paul watched as Liem and Finnlea shared a look. "Anything that you two want to tell me?"

They both shook their heads. The information that Lorcan had provided to them was unproven in their eyes. If Paul was to receive it, it should come from Lorcan, not them.

"What did Lorcan give you?" Paul knew the brothers well enough that he was confident that Lorcan had given Liem some kind of information.

"Ask him. He can explain it to you." Liem walked away, Finnlea's hand tight in his. They needed to be in church that morning, no matter what was happening in their home.

Lorcan slid down into a chair beside Finnlea, his eyes assessing her and then Liem. Something had happened that morning, he could tell.

Liem shook his head at his brother before his eyes dropped to his bride. This was not how he wanted today to be. It looked as if his plans for the day had just walked out of the door. He didn't like it but left it in God's hands.

"We'll talk, Lorcan. Paul is looking for you to find out what you gave us." Liem's voice was kept low.

Lorcan nodded, knowing that Liem would not have given Paul anything of what he had given them.

"I'll find him later. I have a copy of all that for him. I just wanted you to see it first and give me your thoughts. And you will tell me what happened." Lorcan's eyes dropped to Finnlea as she stirred restlessly.

"We will." Liem's attention went back to the front of the church as the worship team began the service. He listened carefully to the message on God's protection, knowing that they were coming into a dangerous time of what they were going through and needed that protection in order to survive.

Finnlea was on her feet as the service ended, pushing at Liem to leave. She just could not stay and greet anyone that morning. Her emotions were too raw from what they had faced earlier that day. Liem's hand was warm and tight on hers as they walked rapidly to his truck. Lorcan trailed after them before he headed for his truck. He was puzzled by their actions.

Liem stood beside Finnlea as they both stared at their front door. They had been reassured that it was safe for them to enter. They just weren't sure that they wanted to. Lorcan stood beside them, not quite sure what was happening but he could tell that something had happened.

"Liem? Talk to me. Tell me why neither one of you are wanting to go in through that door." Lorcan pointed at the door.

"Someone rigged up a wire overnight to both doors. Paul told us that if I had just touched the knob, I would have been electrocuted." Liem was sober as he told his brother what all had transpired that morning.

Lorcan's face paled as he listened to his brother, his eyes on Finnlea's face.

"Finnlea? It's not your fault. You didn't tell them to do that." Lorcan was reading her correctly.

"I know. It just seems odd, that's all. I can't get a sense of why." Finnlea walked through the front door, being careful not to touch anything more than she had to.

Liem followed her, heading for the kitchen. He dropped their Bibles on the countertop before he reached to snap on the coffee pot. Lorcan reached for bread and sandwich fixings. Finnlea watched the brothers work away, knowing that it was years of doing this that had them working as a team. She turned and headed for the office, reaching for the paperwork that had been set there earlier that day.

Finnlea returned to the kitchen, dropping the paperwork on the table and then reaching for plates to set the table. She hugged Liem as she moved past him, finding him hugging her tightly in return. A kiss was dropped on her cheek.

Lorcan shoved aside his plate and reached for the notes on top of the paperwork. He read through the notes before he looked up at his brother.

"You've gone further than I had. What were your thoughts?" Lorcan waited patiently for Finnlea to respond.

"We have. I think that this goes back to my parents. Only I don't know why." Finnlea blinked rapidly.

Chapter 39

Finnlea tapped at the papers that Lorcan still held. Her eyes were on Liem as she did so. He was nodding. They needed to correlate all the information that they had and that Emma had provided to them. He reached to sort through the paperwork, setting it into different piles.

"Lorcan, what were you looking for in what you found?" Finnlea's voice held hope that he could explain his investigation.

"I'm not sure, Finnlea. I am really not sure. I was working from the photos that you received. And then worked backwards from them. I still have some information to confirm." Lorcan looked down for a moment. "I'm sorry, Finnlea. I wish that I could find your parents for you."

Finnlea nodded before she was on her feet, heading for the door as the doorbell rang. She opened it to find Abe and Emma standing there. Emma reached to hug Finnlea before Abe did as well. He then turned and walked around the house. He sensed the danger that was approaching the couple and wanted to ensure that they were as safe as they could be.

"Finnlea? I received your text message. I see that your aunt and uncle are just arriving. We should not be descending on newlyweds like this." Emma moved Finnlea towards the kitchen. "Talk to me, Finnlea."

"We will, Emma. First, let's spend some time in prayer. We need that." Finnlea reached for Liem's hand as she sat beside him, watching Emma and Abe closely and then her aunt and uncle.

After they had spent time in prayer, Liem raised his head, feeling somewhat more confident that they would find the people responsible. He had his doubts that the woman was responsible. He knew her reputation in town and the fact that she liked to be part of the news even if it didn't involve her.

Emma hesitated for a moment, totally unlike her. Abe's arm rested across her shoulders. She knew that he was praying for them all.

"Finnlea. I have a letter here from the government. They have been in touch with the country that you assumed your parents went to. You were correct. What we have discovered is that there was a boating accident. Bodies were recovered but no identification was found. They have now identified your parents. I'm sorry." Emma slid the letter across the table to Finnlea. "Talk to me when you are able to."

Heartbroken sobs shook Finnlea's body as Liem turned her into his arms. His own tears wet her hair. Sara was wrapped in Fergus' arms as they too struggled with their emotions.

Finnlea looked up after a while, finding Emma reading through the paperwork on the table. She moved slightly from Liem's arms.

"Emma? What are your thoughts?" Liem spoke for everyone in the room, knowing that Emma had made some decisions about the material.

Emma looked up at him, assessing him. She nodded. Liem was correct. She had made some decisions.

"This woman? She's not really involved." Emma watched as Liem nodded. "She's trying to become involved but she's being rebuffed. I think that you have already come to that conclusion, haven't you? She is still dangerous to you. If she can take you captive, she will turn you over to the people who are behind this.

"Finnlea, those photos? I think that someone has been following you for their own reasons, not connected to what you are now facing. That is the sense that we are coming to realize. The store? The assaults? What happened this morning? And I do know about it. Paul reached out to Abe and asked for advice on how to keep you two safe."

"That was bizarre. Liem just couldn't go out that door and he wouldn't let me go out o the back door." Finnlea turned to face Liem. "I know God does things like that. I just never expected it to happen to us."

"God does work that way, Finnlea." Abe spoke up. "We've had that experience over the years with our team. And you listened to Him. A lot of people don't and suffer the consequences."

"I agree, Abe." Fergus spoke for the first time. "There have been times that I felt God nudging me.

185

Sometimes I have ignored it and suffered the consequences as you state. He doesn't want us to come to harm."

"He does only want the best for us. We need to listen to Him. It's tough as humans to do that. We want to be in charge of our own lives. It's hard to take our hands off the steering wheel as they say." Abe grinned for a moment.

Emma had been watching Sara closely.

"Sara? You have a thought?"

Sara nodded slowly. She had been awake in the night, thinking back through the years. She remembered a man who had seemed to be really interested in what had happened to Flynn and Leah.

"There was a man who came around a few months after Flynn and Leah disappeared. He would ask questions about them. Neither Fergus nor I gave any information. He stopped abruptly but I always felt as if we were being watched. Fergus and I discussed this over the years and could come to no clear decision about him. Did we do something wrong?"

Emma shook her head. This could be a portion of what Finnlea was now facing. She was convinced that someone was trying to take Liem out of the picture to get to Finnlea. They just didn't have that one piece of information that would solve this. And solve this they needed to. It was obvious that whoever it was behind it was willing to kill Liem to get him out of the way.

Finnlea sighed. This was just getting to be too much for her. And she was tired of it all. She wanted it over and over yesterday.

Chapter 40

Liem reached for the letter, reading it and then staring at it. He was puzzled by the terse tone and lack of any real information.

"Emma? How much have you looked into this?" Liem looked over at her and found her nodding at him.

"You've picked up on what I did. I have someone heading that way to investigate. It may be that we don't find anything or we may find something. It is possible that all identification was lost. I can't see that for a man. His wallet would have been in his pocket." She looked around at a sound from Fergus. "Fergus?"

"Flynn always had his wallet in his right front pocket. And he made sure that it was tucked down deep. It would not have just come out of his pocket. I could see someone taking it and taking the money and tossing the wallet." Fergus was distressed at the thought.

"We'll look into everything that we can." Emma was on her feet, knowing that they need to head for home. "Don't worry, Finnlea, Liem. We will keep you informed every step of the way. I am praying that I have more news today."

Finnlea turned back from the door after locking it. She could hear the conversation in the kitchen and realized that Lora had joined the group by coming in the back door. Finnlea leaned against the door, her thoughts troubled. She didn't understand why her. That was where the key lay, she decided. She walked back through the house to the office and stared at the computer before she headed back to the kitchen.

Standing for a moment and staring at her groom, Finnlea finally nodded. There was more to the story, as they say, she decided. Fergus was on his feet, moving in on her and giving her a hug before he stood back with his hands on her shoulders.

"Finnlea? What are you thinking?" Fergus knew that she had come to a conclusion.

"I am thinking that there is something else out there. This with Mom and Dad? It's a smoke screen. We've looked into everything about them. We haven't looked into you and Aunt Sara. Who hates you enough to destroy your family, even though I am just your niece?" Finnlea could hear the conversation stopping in the room.

Liem was on his feet, his arm around his wife. She had just voiced the thought that he had been considering for the last few days and didn't know how to approach her or Fergus.

Fergus stared at her, feeling Sara's hand on his back.

"Why would you say that?" Fergus could barely speak.

"Someone hates you enough to get rid of Mom and Dad. They knew that you would take me in. If they could destroy me, then they would destroy you." Finnlea was adamant in her words. She felt that she was on the right track. She looked up, not surprised to find Paul standing just inside the doorway. "Paul? Is this the key that you need?"

Paul nodded, realizing that Finnlea had indeed provided the key to the puzzle. He had only given Fergus a quick look. That would change now. Paul had to agree with Finnlea. It had never made sense about her parents.

"I think it is, Finnlea. I agree with you that it has never made sense about your parents. Let me have a few days. Fergus, you and I need to sit down and have a real heart to heart."

Fergus was nodding. Paul was correct. They did need to sit down and have a long conversation. He wanted Sara to be part of it. He pointed towards the table.

"Sit, Paul. I want everyone in on this conversation." Fergus seated his wife and then reached to make more coffee. "It's going to be a long conversation, I think."

Fergus was right in his assessment. It was an afternoon-long conversation. Finnlea was not surprised to hear what her uncle had to say. Sara looked distressed at times but she was in full support of her husband's words. Paul asked the questions that he needed to before he tucked away his notepad and rose. He was gone before anyone could say anything.

That evening, Liem found Finnlea curled up on the couch, a blanket wrapped around her. He simply sat beside her and wrapped her into a hug. His audible prayer helped to calm her emotions. He didn't say anything other than to pray for her.

"Will this solve it?" Finnlea's voice was almost too quiet to be heard. She was afraid to ask.

Liem shrugged, not sure what to say.

"I pray that it does. Paul will do his best on this. I sent Emma an email not that long ago, just to update her on what we talked about. She had already had that thought and had been working on it. She hasn't found anything yet but with more names that Fergus provided, she'll widen her search."

"I am sure that she will. This makes more sense that Mom and Dad." She grew pensive.

"It does." Liem tilted his head to study his bride. "Are you okay with what Emma said?"

Finnlea shrugged. She was not sure how to feel. It was something that she had to work through with God.

"I'm not sure, love. I really am. Not sure. God and I are having conversations about it." Finnlea leaned against Liem. "This is not how we're supposed to start our marriage."

Liem grinned at that. She had echoed his thoughts.

"No, it's not but it is how God has directed our steps. He uses people to bring others to justice. Abe has been telling me about their friends and others that he knows and what they went through."

"I just wish He had chosen someone else." She sighed. "I'm sorry, Lord. I know that You are in control. I just wish it had been different." She nestled down on Liem and drifted off to sleep.

Liem studied her face and kissed her before his head was down on his bride's and he slept. Neither heard the slight movement around the house nor the whispered words as the men tried to find a way in. No way in was found and they left frustrated. They were under orders to bring Liem to their boss. He was to be used to bring Fergus to heel, as it was said, using Finnlea against Fergus.

Chapter 41

Finnlea stared at Paul the next morning. He had tracked her down at her store even though it wasn't open for business. She had let him in and then locked the door behind him. Frustration was evident on her face.

"Paul? How am I supposed to do my inventory and online orders if you keep showing up?" She was disgruntled and wasn't afraid to let it show.

Paul laughed at her. He knew that she was just grumping at him as Lora would have said. He pointed at the counter where she had paperwork spread out.

"I'm sorry. I know that I am interrupting you. How can I help?" He dropped his portfolio on the counter.

"By going away? By solving this? I don't know. I just want this over. Liem didn't deserve to be drawn into this, whatever this is."

Paul was nodding. He had already tracked Liem down at his jobsite. Liem's words had a bite to them, something that was unusual for him. That told Paul how much under stress that his friend was. Paul wanted it over for his friend as well. He felt selfish. He wanted it over for himself as well. He had watched Liem and Finnlea and then had turned to find a lady of his own. This case was taking a lot from him and he wanted it over so that he could date the lady that God had brought into his life. Paul also knew that Lorcan and Eve were dating and that both felt constrained by what was facing Liem and Finnlea.

Finnlea looked contrite and her mouth opened to apologize. It snapped closed as Paul shook his head. Paul wandered the shop, taking in the articles for sale. Finnlea had reached out to the artists in the neighbourhood in just a few short weeks and had expanded their reach to customers. She had that personality, he realized.

Watching Paul as he walked through her store, Finnlea sighed. She was almost done with her work for the day and had planned on heading to the grocery store and then the bakeshop. She wanted to have a special meal waiting for Liem when he came home. She just didn't know if she could now.

"Paul? You're here for a reason." Finnlea stopped beside him. Her work was put neatly away. She was thankful for Lora, who had taken on the online store and was running away with it. It was making a profit, something that she had not expected as of yet.

"I am, Finnlea. First, how are you?" Paul watched with compassion as his friend's eyes closed and a single tear trickled down her cheek.

"I don't know, Paul. I'm not sure how to feel. I want this over. I can feel the danger reaching out more and more towards us. If I knew why or who, it would make it easier." Finnlea stared out of the front window of the store, thinking that Paul would censure her.

"That's totally understandable, Finnlea. All victims of crime have those feelings at some point or other. It's not unusual. Just know that you are not alone in this. Nor is Liem. We are with you. Our officers are working to try and find the villain. I don't know if you were aware that Liem's father and mother were both officers. Leith died on the job from a drunk driver. Lily died from a broken heart, we all say. She suffered a heart attack when the boys were only in college. That devastated them. Lora took on the role of more than an aunt to them at that point."

Finnlea had turned to watch Paul. She was familiar with the facts but not how it was affecting everyone.

"I didn't really that it was so wide spread in trying to solve this." Finnlea bit at her lip. "They must blame me." She frowned at him as he shook his head. "They have to." She sighed. "Paul, go back to work. I know that you don't have anything for me to look at." She shooed him out of the door and then locked it behind them. Paul insisted on walking her to her car.

The sudden revving of an engine and squealing of tires had Paul spinning in a circle and then shoving at Finnlea. He shoved hard enough that she had trouble keeping to her feet. His car door was open as he shoved her inside and then almost slide across the hood to jump behind the wheel. He sped away, leaving dark tire marks behind him on the pavement as with lights and sirens on, he headed for the detachment. He flew through the gate that opened for him before he slammed to a stop. Finnlea was in shock as Paul wrenched open her door and pulled her from the vehicle

"Inside, Finnlea! Now!" His voice barked at her as his hand grasped at her arm and tugged her forward at a run towards the back door of the station. The door opened quickly and then shut just as quickly behind them.

Finnlea shook off his hand and glared at him. There was no excuse, she decided, for how he had treated her. A finger in the air stopped her protests as his hand once more tugged her through the building to his office. He shoved her into a chair, taking with thanks the visitor badge handed to him.

"Put that on." His voice was harsh. A slight glimmer of a smile showed in his eyes as her mouth opened to protest and then snapped shut as she clipped the badge to her jeans. "Thank you."

"What was that all about, Paul?" Finnlea's anger came through in the words that she shot at him.

"Someone was waiting for you." Paul walked from the office, asking the desk officer to send someone to find Liem. He had a bad feeling about his friend's safety. He paused for a moment to pray for wisdom. This was heating up, he decided, and he needed someone to guide his words and his actions. Paul wasn't so confident in his ability to do that sanely any more.

Finnlea was on her feet, her phone in her hand. She had tried to reach Liem and had been unable to do so. She was frantic to know that he was okay.

"Paul? Where is Liem? I can't reach him." She was ready to run past him and run right to where Liem was working.

"I have someone on the way to find him. Back in my office, Finnlea." Paul shoved her back into the room. He turned as he heard his name called and stepped back into the hallway, closing the door behind him.

"Paul? The patrol officer found Liem's truck on the side of the road. It was open. Liem is not in it. We're searching the area." The officer was disturbed by the fact.

Paul had come to that conclusion. He shot a look at the closed office door. He didn't know how he would tell Finnlea that Liem had disappeared. Paul opened his office door, finding Finnlea watching for him, hope on her face. Her face fell at the look on his face.

"He's gone, isn't he? You don't need to say it in words. I can see it on your face." Finnlea buried her face in her hands, her emotions too much for her to even weep.

Chapter 42

Finnlea paced her home that night, missing Liem greatly. She had been escorted home by officers. There were at least two officers outside right now, she knew, and one inside with her. She just hated it. Where was Liem? That question kept playing on her mind.

Hearing Lorcan's voice, Finnlea walked towards the living room, finding Lorcan and Lora staring at her. Lora reached for her and hugged her. Finnlea looked past them to see Fergus and Sara entering as well. She almost ran to Sara, hugging her aunt as tightly as she could. Finnlea sobbed, huge heart-broken sobs. Fergus' arms surrounded his ladies as he termed them. He too was distraught that Liem had gone missing. He wanted to be out there looking for him except that Paul had ordered him to be in this house and not to leave.

Paul looked up from his notes as he sat at his office desk. There had been no sign of Liem, despite the best efforts of the patrol officers. Even the people on the street were looking for him without any success. He hated this. He felt that the couple had been through enough.

"Paul?" His supervisor entered and then just stood and watched him. They had had numerous conversations about this case.

"No word, George. Not one sighting of him. Finnlea's at their home with their relatives. I don't want them separated."

George nodded. It was what he would have done, had it been his case.

"Any sense of why?"

Paul nodded. He was beginning to get a sense of why. It did go back to Fergus after all.

"It goes back to Fergus. We're still retrieving information from that. I don't have the complete sense of why or who."

George thought through what he had been told by Paul and nodded as well. It was coming together. They just had to find Liem before it was too late and Finnlea was left a widow.

Late that evening, Paul trudged towards his house, lost in thought. He didn't hear the running footsteps until he landed forcefully on the ground, face first. His arms were held down even as he struggled to rise. A sharp blow to the back of his head sent him spiralling into darkness. A few minutes later, he was sitting up and pushing his hand at his head. Stumbling to his feet, he stared at the envelope on the ground in front of him. Bending to pick it over almost sent him back to the ground.

Paul locked the door behind him and then stumbled to the kitchen. He reached for an ice pack and slapped it to his head. He stared at the envelope before he opened it with one hand. Paul stared at the watch that tumbled to the table as he turned the envelope upside down. It was Liem's, he knew. He had no idea who had sent it to him.

George shut Paul's front door after him as he followed Paul through the house. He was worried about his detective. He had no idea what was happening other than that Paul had been hurt.

"I got that. It's Liem's watch." Paul pointed at the table. "I was attacked as I walked from my car. I didn't see or hear anything." Paul was frustrated at that.

"It is?" George stared down at it. "They're sending a message to you."

"And I don't know why to me and not to Finnlea."

"They can't get to her. They can to you. But why?" George paced the room, scenarios running through his min.

"I know that they can't. I just fear for his life."

"There is that. We need to find him and quickly." George stared around before he reached for the pad of paper and pen that sat on the kitchen counter. He sat at the table, making notes.

"I know that we do. I just don't know where they would take him." Paul sat as well, rubbing at the back of his head.

"That's a good question. We have an idea of who has taken him. We need to search for all the properties that they own. And there are a lot."

"There are. I have no idea which one to start with." Paul dropped his head into his hands. It was aching badly and making it difficult for him to think.

———

George left at last, Paul standing on his front porch and studying the night sky. He was praying fervently for information as to where Liem was. He knew that Liem was in God's hands but he still worried about him.

Finnlea tossed and turned restlessly that night. Her sleep was filled with dreams or nightmares as she declared in the morning. Liem and his disappearance dominated them. She woke in the morning, drenched in sweat and terrified for her groom. On her feet and dressed, Finnlea reached to pour herself a mug of coffee and then headed for the office. She reached for the papers that had been printed off the night before. She had been too distraught to look through them at the time but now she was ready to. With a highlighter in hand, Finnlea began to read them and then she began to highlight points and information that stood out to her.

Lorcan paused as he passed the door to the office before he returned with his own mug of coffee in his hand. He reached for the papers that she was setting to one side, reading through them and taking note of what she had highlighted. He was not surprised that she was picking up on the importance of what she was indicating. He looked up to find her watching him.

"Lorcan? What do you see in this?" Finnlea waited for him to speak, hoping and praying that he had seen what she had.

"I'm seeing something here, Finnlea." He looked around as he heard footsteps and Fergus appeared in the doorway. "Fergus?"

"You two are up early. Finnlea?" Fergus studied his niece, seeing the devastation on her face.

"It's okay, Uncle Fergus." She waited for him to sit before she looked down at the desk. "Uncle Fergus? I need to ask you something and I'm not quite sure how to word it." She struggled with her emotions and thoughts. "We've been trying to prove that someone died who you were treating. I mean, both you and Aunt Sara are retired paramedics. What if it isn't someone who died? What if someone lived who was supposed to die and didn't? And it goes back to before I came to live with you?"

Fergus stared at his niece, shock on his face. He could hear Lorcan murmuring beside him.

"You mean this?" At Finnlea's nod, he sat back, still trying to take in what her question meant.

Chapter 42

Paul stared in shock at Finnlea as she kept shoving papers at him. He appeared that afternoon, anxious about Finnlea. He had not expected to find her surrounded by piles of paper or that the others would be deep in the investigation as well. Lora had disappeared to run the store for Finnlea.

"What did you say?" Paul wasn't quite sure that he had heard her correctly.

"That it was someone who didn't die when they should have. Uncle Fergus kept them alive. We've been going back over what he can remember. We'll need you to request the information in a formal way." Finnlea spun away from him, energy sparking from her that none of them had seen for a few days. "Whoever this is has taken Liem to get to me. If he can get to me, then he can get to Uncle Fergus."

Nodding, Paul found a seat and read through the paperwork that had been thrust at him. Finnlea was good, he decided, knowing that she had worked through this with her family. And that disturbed him.

Fergus watched Finnlea closely. He knew her better than anyone in the room, other than Sara. He could see how close to the edge that she was but also knew that she would not give up until she collapsed. He would try and prevent that but he didn't think that it would be possible. A look on Finnlea's face drew Fergus to his feet and reaching for the papers in her hand. He dropped them on the table before he had

Finnlea on her feet and walking from the room, despite her protests.

"I need to work on that, Uncle Fergus." Finnlea struggled to return to the office.

"No, you need a break. You're fragile right now, Finnlea. Come and sit outside with me. We'll pray through what we're discovering. And then we'll go back at it for a while refreshed. God is in control, love."

Finnlea sighed as she sat down in a chair on the deck. She was frustrated and more than a little worried about Liem.

"I know, Uncle Fergus. It just doesn't feel as if He is." Her eyes closed as she struggled with the tears that threatened to overwhelm her. "I can't do this."

"Not in your own strength, Finnlea. This is where you are called to God and called to your Protector. He is that, you know. He is in control and only wants the best for both you and Liem. Sometimes, it just doesn't seem as if he does."

Finnlea had turned her head to watch her uncle and saw that Sara had followed them outside. Sara reached to hug her niece, her own prayer whispering in the silence.

"Will this work, do you think?" Finnlea was grasping at the proverbial straw, praying that she would find the one piece of information that would bring the villain as she thought of him out into the open.

"We'll make it work, Finnlea." Paul had appeared. "You've done a lot of work for us already, all of you. Lorcan has provided what information he can that I have an officer working on verifying. That's how we do it." He leaned forward, his elbows planted on his knees. "We'll find Liem for you."

"I know that you will. I just don't know if he'll be alive or dead." Sobs shook her body. She was stretched past what she thought and knew that she could handle. Only God could give her the strength and will to continue.

"We pray that he is alive, Finnlea." Paul reached for his phone, a frown on his face before he excused himself. Duty and another investigation were taking him away from where he really wanted to be.

Finnlea watched him walk away, praying for their friend. He was stressed, she could tell, and knew that only God would be able to relieve that stress.

Fergus sat back, thinking through the cases and patients that he had been part of treating over the years. He was puzzled at Finnlea's words but trusted her instincts enough to go with what she had suggested. His eyes slid closed. He knew who it was. With his phone in his hand, Fergus walked away to send a text to Paul. He turned to watch Finnlea before he sent a text to Emma, asking her to investigate that person and whoever might be related to him. He was confident that he had determined the patient. They just had to find his family. And that family would be in this town. He had no doubt about that.

Watching her uncle, Finnlea was discouraged. She thought that Fergus had come to a conclusion but she wasn't sure at all. She just wanted this all over with.

Sara's arm tightened around her niece. Her gaze shifted between her niece and her husband. Fergus' eyes met hers and he nodded. She sighed at the thought that he had determined who it was.

Fergus sat back down beside Finnlea, his arm around her. He prayed for her, studying Finnlea as he did so. He wanted to relieve her worry but he didn't quite know how to do that.

"Finnlea? I think that I know who it is. I have asked Paul and Emma to investigate this person. I will tell you the name. If it is this person, then we need to come up with something that will protect you. And I fear that we won't be able to protect you."

"You're doing God's work, Uncle Fergus. He will protect me when no one else can. I have to trust myself and Liem to His care. I need to trust Him but I have to." Finnlea blinked rapidly. She was exhausted, not having slept much the night before.

"I know that I am, Finnlea. It's how we do this, you know?" Fergus gave a small smile. "Now, let's head in and find our lunch and then we'll continue to work on this." He looked up as Lorcan appeared. "Lorcan?"

"It's okay. I needed a break. Did someone mention food?" He grinned at Fergus before he was on his feet and headed back into the house to find something for them to eat.

Chapter 43

A day later, Finnlea wandered her store before Eve sent her home. She wasn't accomplishing anything there, she knew, but she also didn't want to be alone. She felt a sense of doom and gloom as her aunt would have said. Sighing, she sat at her kitchen table, a mug of tea this time in front of her. Finnlea had tidied away all the papers the night before, not wanting to even think about them.

Her head bowed as she petitioned God to bring Liem home to her. She had to accept the fact that she might not like how he came back. His life was in God's hands. That much she knew. She looked up as she heard a tap at the front door and rose.

Lorcan studied Finnlea, seeing the stress and fatigue that she was trying so hard to hide. He gave her a quick hug on the way by. He had felt such an urgent nudge from God that morning and knew that Finnlea should not be on her own. Her aunt and uncle had flown out that morning on a business trip and would not be back for at least three days. That didn't help, he decided.

"Lorcan? What are you doing here?" Finnlea simply stared at him as he sat across from her. She had come to love Lorcan as the brother that she had never had.

"You need me here, Finnlea. God told me that. I don't know why but I will not go contrary to His nudge."

"Thank you, Lorcan. I am afraid this morning and I don't know why. Your girlfriend sent me home. She told me that I was just stirring up dust and it would be up to her to clean it up. She would rather not have to do that." Finnlea grinned as Lorcan laughed.

"She told you that, did she?"

Finnlea had taken her seat again facing the door. She looked up as she heard a key in the door and then the sound of familiar footsteps. Liem was home! Her face glowed with eagerness to see him and her love for him. As she started to rise, her face changed. It became stressed and fear covered. Lorcan stared at her and then too began to rise before he felt the nudge of a gun barrel on the back of his neck. He froze in place, his hands raised in the air.

Sitting back in her chair, Finnlea's eyes did not move from Liem. She studied his beloved face, seeing the worry and fear that he was trying so hard to hide. She also saw the dark, dark circles under his eyes and that he was swaying slightly from fatigue.

Her eyes did not move from him even though she sensed other men moving around the room. She jumped as she felt hands on her shoulders, holding her in place. She whimpered slightly at the tight hold before her focus shifted back to Liem.

Liem watched his beloved bride, unable to get to her. He had been warned and warned severely that if he made a move that would indicate he was trying to get free, his bride would be harmed. He had nodded slowly, his brain feeling foggy from lack of sleep and lack of food. It had been rough with him the last few days and he wanted to preserve what energy and strength he had to protect his lady. Sure, he knew that God was protecting them. That didn't change the fact that he felt he had to do that. Only, Liem didn't know how he would do that. The five men in the room with them would prevent that.

Lorcan could sense that the men were waiting for someone. He sighed to himself. There was no way that either he or Liem would be able to take on the five men. He knew that Finnlea would be in there, helping them despite the fact that she was a lady. It was who she was. That would make it worse for Liem as he would certainly come to her aid.

Finnlea's gaze shifted to watch the man standing behind Liem. She frowned for a moment. He certainly didn't fit her idea of the men who had taken her groom hostage. Finnlea saw the slight negative shake of his head and frowned harder. Her eyes went back to Liem, finding him watching her intently, his love for her shining in his eyes.

"What do you want?" Finnlea took the initiative and spoke. She felt the hands tighten on her shoulders. "You're in our home. At the very least, you can tell us why." Her tongue found the cut on her lip and she tasted the salty coppery blood in her mouth. That was a real smart move, she decided.

Liem growled at the treatment that Finnlea had just taken but a hand on his shoulder kept him in place. He settled back on his feet, his fatigue and lack of food dulling his senses. He would have to wait for an opportunity to act. Liem could see that Lorcan had gathered himself up, ready to attack if the opportunity presented itself. And it would. The men were growing careless, he knew, confident that he would not act out in any way for fear that Finnlea would be hurt. He snorted to himself. They didn't know his bride. He was just afraid that she would act without warning and be seriously hurt or killed.

Finnlea shifted on her chair. She knew that the men were waiting for someone to appear. She just wanted to know who was behind the men. And Finnlea was well aware that they would be unable to call for any help. It would be up to the three of them to overcome the men and release themselves. Her eyes shifted as they followed the men pacing their home. The man behind Lorcan and herself didn't move. She sought the man again behind Liem, finding him watching the men who were holding them captive and not the captive themselves. She frowned once more. He had to be undercover, she decided. He doesn't want to see the three of them hurt but he wasn't ready to play his hand yet.

"Again, what do you want? And just who are you waiting for? It's obvious that none of you are in charge." Finnlea just stared back at the man, not letting him see how scared that she was.

"Be quiet!" The man's hand was raised again before he stopped abruptly and then dropped his hand. They all could see a puzzled look on his face for a moment before he backed away from Finnlea and then just stood staring at her.

Chapter 44

Afterwards, it seemed as if hours had passed and even a night and day had gone by. It really wasn't that long, they all decided. The increasing sense of danger had weighed on the three who were held captive. They had no idea who the men were waiting for.

Liem had continued to stand, not allowed to sit or even lean against the wall. He didn't know how long he could continue to stand. He had not been allowed to sleep. And he had only been given water to drink and that only in a small amount. His worry for Finnlea had driven him to pace the room that he had been imprisoned in. No matter how many times he had questioned the men, he had received no response. He had struggled to escape and had been forced back into the room.

The night that he had been taken captive, Liem had been heading for Finnlea's store. He was eager to find her and then take her out for a meal. He didn't make it far from his work before his truck was boxed in on all sides and he was forced to a stop. Liem refused to open his window or door until the gun was pointed at him and the trigger cocked. He shoved open his door and dropped to the ground. Forced into one of the trucks, Liem had stared out at his truck, seeing his door shoved shut before the trucks that had surrounded him drive away.

Shoved into a house, Liem had stood, not moving, not sure what was happening. He wasn't moved from that room unless he needed to and then he was put right back in there. Liem had not seen the men's employer even as he had demanded that. He sighed to himself more than once and he could only pray for his bride. She was in God's hands and under his protection.

Lorcan kept his eyes on the men, his muscles tense and ready to jump to his feet and attack them. He too had picked up the demeanour of the man behind Liem. He had been unable to catch his brother's eyes. He didn't blame his brother for not taking his eyes off of his lady. Lorcan knew that he would have done the same had it been Eve instead of Finnlea.

The man who seemed to be in charge paced away from them, his phone in his hand. He read the text message from his employer and grew angry. He spun to start at Finnlea, blaming her. He had just found out that her aunt and uncle had left the province and would not be back for three days. What were they to do until they returned?

The other men watched him, seeing his anger. They shared a look with one another before they looked at the three captives. They frowned. None of the captives showed any fear or discomfort. The men could not understand that. They didn't know that God had granted the three His peace and comfort.

Finnlea's eyes followed the men before she was on her feet, heading for the kitchen. A hand on her arm abruptly stopped her and she heard a growl of protest from Liem.

"Get back in your chair!"

"No. We need to eat and you will not stop me from preparing something. I can tell that you starved Liem." Finnlea's hand rested on her cheek as she stared up at the man. A cruel blow had taken her to the floor. She could hear Liem's protests in the background. "Did you really have to do that? Who's going to feed you now?" Finnlea was on her feet and in the man's face. "I certainly won't be preparing anything for you."

The man shoved her back into her chair. His hand landed heavily on her shoulder preventing her from rising even though she struggled to rise.

"What is your problem?" Finnlea managed to spin on her seat, glaring at the man.

"You stay in your chair." The man pointed at Lorcan. "He gets water for you. That's all you get."

Lorcan rose carefully, being cautious not to move rapidly or in a threatening manner. He returned from the kitchen with three bottles of water, handing one to Finnlea, one to Liem, and then sat back down. He wasn't sure what to expect but somehow he didn't think that they would be allowed much more than water. His eyes found Liem and he frowned harder. His brother could hardly stand but he was not allowed to sit. Somehow, Lorcan didn't think that Liem would be on his feet much longer.

Finnlea twisted the bottle of water in her hands. It would not serve as a weapon, she could tell that. She looked around and frowned. Two of the men stepped out of the room. She thought that she had heard the front door close quietly. She looked at Liem and sighed. He was on the verge of collapsing and she was afraid that he would do just that and hurt himself.

Liem found himself swaying more and more. He just could not stop his motions. He sighed to himself and then prayed for strength. His eyes rolled backwards and Liem slumped to the floor, the sound of his body hitting the wooden floor loud in the room. He didn't hear Finnlea scream and then scramble away from the man who tried to grasp her hair.

Finnlea was on her knees beside Liem, frantically trying to turn him over and feel for a pulse. The man who had been guarding Liem was on the floor beside her, his hands reaching to help.

"Is he dead?" The man who stood behind Lorcan voiced the question that no one else was willing to ask.

"He is not. He's unconscious." Finnlea spun on her knees. "I need to get him off the floor." She picked herself up once more, her hand on her mouth. This had to stop, she decided. It would do Liem no good if she kept getting herself beaten.

Lorcan was on his feet, his hands fisted. He was ready to defend his brother's lady but the gun pointed at him stopped his forward motion. He looked around and frowned. Like Finnlea, he was sure that he had heard the front door close. Lorcan spun, taking the man behind him by surprise. His nodded fist connected with the man's jaw, sending him to the floor where he lay motionless. He heard Finnlea scream and ducked the fist heading his way. His fist seemed to almost rise from the floor as he directed it upward at the man. The man was unable to avoid it and landed beside his friend on the floor.

Flying to the door, Lorcan locked it and shoved home the dead bolt before he was back beside his brother. His hand reached across Liem to rest on Finnlea's shoulder for a moment before he was calling for assistance.

The man who had been watching Liem reached to tie up the other two men. He shook his head at Lorcan who was staring at him in surprise. He had not picked up that the man was trying to help them.

Chapter 45

Paul strode rapidly into the hospital, his eyes searching for his friends. The charge nurse pointed to a room, a slight smile on his face. He paused outside of the door, hearing Finnlea protesting at something. She's back and in fine form, he decided. Shoving open the door, Paul stood for a moment and watched Finnlea as she faced off against a nurse. He caught the amused look that Lorcan was trying hard to hide.

Moving into the room, Paul's hand landed on Finnlea's shoulder, causing her to jump and stare at him with fear. She then frowned at him.

"Finnlea? Have you been seen to yet?" Paul studied her face.

"No. Not until Liem is seen to. And I am not leaving him. Not for one moment." Finnlea spun away from Paul and stalked back to stand at Liem's side, a hand resting on his face.

The nurse was not happy with Finnlea, that much was obvious. Paul's hand on her arm drew her from the room. He stopped just outside the door, watching as the charge nurse appeared. He also watched the patrol officer who had come to stand near the door.

"Nurse? These people stay together. That is not an option." Paul was angry at the reaction from the nurse. He looked at the charge nurse. "They are under police protection and we are not going to separate them. If you can't accept that, then I suggest your supervisor replace you."

The charge nurse pointed at the nurse and then motioned her to walk away. This was not the first time that one of the supervisors had had to speak with her. This would be the last time.

"Detective? There is no issue with them staying together. I know Liem and Lorcan and was in on the search for Liem. I'll find another nurse to take care of them." She walked away, leaving Paul staring at the wall across from him before he turned back into the room.

Lorcan looked around from where he had planted his feet at the end of the stretcher. Paul approached Finnlea, tilting his head to study the bruises on her face and the cut on her lip. She didn't look up at him. Her focus was slowly on Liem.

Paul walked away at last, Finnlea's keys in his hand. She had given them to him at his request, simply handing them to him without asking any questions. He could tell how worried that she was. He beckoned to Lorcan who followed him from the room.

"Lorcan? What happened? I know that you have given your statements, other than for Liem."

"Liem just showed up this morning. There were five men with him." Lorcan was puzzled at that. "They seemed to be waiting for someone to appear. Only no one else did. A while ago, two of the men left. Liem collapsed and that's when I was able to take down two of the men. They're in custody. There was one man though who didn't seem to fit in. He tried to help Liem when he collapsed. Finnlea maintains that he was an undercover officer."

Paul's hand paused for a moment as he was making his notes. That was something that he would need to look into and that he would do as soon as he could. He looked around the home, not finding anything that seemed odd.

"What else?"

Lorcan shrugged. He stared at the spot where Liem had collapsed to the floor and then had not moved. He was deeply worried about his brother even though he knew that God was taking care of him.

"Not much else. Finnlea didn't back down from them." Lorcan grinned suddenly. "She even decided that she needed to make us all a meal. That didn't go over very well."

"No, I don't expect that it would." Paul locked the door behind them. "We're closing in on the main villain, Lorcan. It will be a few days. Can you keep your sister-in-law out of trouble? I'm told that Liem will be admitted for at least the night."

"He is to be admitted. Finnlea will not leave him, that much I know." Lorcan sighed. He was exhausted.

"No, I don't want her to." Paul pulled to a stop in front of the hospital. "Get some rest, Lorcan. You're wearing out."

Lorcan walked into the room on the medical floor to find Finnlea curled up in a chair as close as she could get to Liem. She was asleep. He looked then at his brother, seeing that some colour had come back into his white face. He prayed for them before he turned and walked away, heading for his truck and then to find Eve. Lorcan just needed to see his lady.

Finnlea was on her feet not that long afterwards, hearing the soft moans coming from Liem. He was starting to rouse and was muttering to himself about Finnlea and the danger that she was in.

Her hand rested against Liem's cheek, feeling the stubble under it. He turned his face into it, his eyes flickering open and closed. His tongue came out to wet his lips as he tried to speak.

"Finnlea? Is that you?" His voice was hoarse and he tried hard to swallow.

"It is, love. It is. Don't move. They want you to lie quiet." Finnlea struggled to keep Liem, a losing battle.

"I need to find Finnlea. She's in danger. I need to get up." Liem sat up and then abruptly slumped back on the pillow. His eyes closed as he dropped off into a natural sleep.

The nurse had approached as this had transpired. She checked the intravenous line and fluid and then smiled at Finnlea.

"It's okay, Finnlea. He'll do this likely for a few times. It's normal. Can I get you anything?"

Finnlea shook her head. Everyone was taking care of her, she decided, and that wasn't the way it was supposed to be. She studied Liem, feeling the fatigue drawing her down into its grasp. Finnlea simply crawled up to lie beside him, her arm stretched out across his chest. She slept, not feeling Liem moving his arm and wrapping it around her.

Chapter 46

The man stood outside of the hospital, staring up at it. His eyes showed his rage and anger even though he kept it from his face. He was angry that for some reason the two had escaped his men. They could not explain it to him. The two that had been taken down by Lorcan were still in jail, refusing to talk to the investigators. The third man had disappeared and he wanted him.

The man's gaze shifted to the couple walking past him and his face tightened further with his anger. He followed them, not seeing Paul approaching him. Paul looked around, beckoning to the officers who had just appeared. He pointed towards the man and they nodded.

Paul caught up with Fergus and Sara as they waited for the elevator, pointing instead to the stairs. They frowned at him and then followed him as he headed for the stairwell. They rapidly climbed to the medical floor. Paul shoved open the door and then pointed to Liem's room.

"In there. And stay there until I come for you." Paul walked rapidly towards the nurse's desk, stopping to speak with the charge nurse.

Fergus and Sara stared at one another and then headed for Liem's room. The officer shoved the door open for them and then moved to stand right in front of it, another officer standing across the hall from him.

Finnlea didn't rouse as her aunt and uncle walked towards the bed but Liem did. His eyes opened as he stared around the room, disoriented for a moment. His gaze landed on Fergus and Sara before his frown disappeared.

"Fergus? Sara? What? Where am I?"

"You're in the hospital, Liem. I don't know what all happened but Paul called us to come back, that Finnlea and you needed us. We came back as soon as we could. You're free and home!" Fergus wrapped an arm around Sara as she struggled with her emotions.

"I am." Liem's head went back against the pillow, his eyes on Finnlea who still slept. "I'm not sure how I ended up here but I am grateful that God freed me. We'll talk about it later." Liem slept once more, leaving Fergus and Sara to stare at one another.

Paul walked back towards the officers, sending one to stand inside the room and the other officer to stand near the nurse's station. He himself walked into the room and then stood near the window, hidden to view somewhat.

The door creaked slowly open and stopped partway before it was shoved all the way open. The man who entered glared at Fergus as he spun to stare at the man. Fergus shoved Sara behind him as he stood his ground, prepared to defend his family.

"So, it's you. I wondered if it was." Fergus didn't wait for the man to speak. He watched as the officer approached the man from behind and then stood and waited for Paul's signal to take the man into custody.

"Of course, it is. I've been watching you for years. That woman there has been my link to watching you. She's to pay for what you did." Warren Gibson sneered at the man that he had been following for years, just waiting for the opportunity to destroy him. To his mind, that time had arrived.

"Gibson? Your son? You tried to kill him. I have no idea why but God didn't mean for him to die. I have kept in touch with him over the years. He is a good man who serves his God as a pastor. You, on the other hand, serve the devil and always have."

This incensed Gibson. A weapon appeared in his hand that he pointed directly at Finnlea. Finnlea had roused and raised herself to a sitting position, Liem's eyes on Gibson as his arm surrounded his bride.

Gibson's hand shook with the strength of his anger. He wanted to kill all four that were in front of him but he didn't know who to shoot first. The officer standing behind him moved it and gripped the man's hand, preventing Gibson from shooting anyone. The weapon dropped to the floor and then spun away from him. Handcuffs snapped on Gibson's wrists even as he struggled to escape. He was led away, almost anti-climatically as Paul approached Fergus.

"It's over, Finnlea. Fergus, we have the man who has followed you for years. He wanted his son dead because he didn't like him. There was no other reason for that decision. You saved him after the accident. Gibson held that against you. When you took in Finnlea and raised her, he decided that he would use her as a weapon against you. We'll meet again to finalize everything."

Paul walked away with the four in the room staring after him. Finnlea was off the bed to hug her uncle. Fergus held on to her for a little bit longer than normal before he handed her off to Sara. He then turned to Liem, finding that man sitting up in bed, watching Finnlea closely.

"Liem, I'm sorry."

"You're sorry? It's not your fault. It's his. He is evil and chose that path. You did nothing wrong. God protected you, Sara, and Finnlea through the years. He has also chosen you to bring Gibson to justice." Liem reached for Finnlea, wrapping her in his arms as she wept, the burden gone from her.

Chapter 47

A week later, Finnlea turned away from locking the front door as their guests had left. She found Liem standing there, waiting with his arms open to wrap her into a tight hug. He was well once more physically. Emotionally, he was struggling with what had happened to him.

"Okay, sweetheart?" Liem kissed her before his chin rested on the top of her head.

"I am. Thank you, Liem, for being who you are. God has blessed me with the man who is just right for me." She hugged him tight before she shoved away from him.

Sara, Lora, and Eve had helped them clear away the mess from the meal that they had shared before Paul had taken the floor and just finished off what he needed to tell them or could tell them.

Paul had prayed for his friends before he spoke. It had simply come down to the fact that Fergus had done what he was trained to do and saved a life. Gibson's son was to have died. His father had no other reason to give other than that he didn't like him and didn't want him. He had lived a life of crime and that list of crimes was growing daily. Paul had found the undercover officer and spoken with him, simply letting him walk away when they were done. He could not share with these friends what had been said. He had also explained that the man had been killed in Finnlea's store as a threat. Everything that had been directed at them had come from Gibson.

Finnlea had looked sad at that. She had heard from Emma that her parents' bodies could be returned to this country if she wanted. She had said that she would think about it. Emma had confirmed that it had been a simple boating accident that had taken their lives.

Liem had held his bride as Paul spoke, his head resting against hers. They had spent many hours talking over what had happened. Finnlea was sharing with her groom the feelings that she had hidden over the years. He prayed for her and wept with her. God had protected them, they both acknowledged. He had been their Protector and He had called them to run to Him.

"Liem? I need to get away for a few days." Finnlea walked away from Liem.

He followed her, his hand stopping her forward walk.

"We do. It's a long weekend. How be we head north for a bit and find somewhere we can stay that's not too close to civilization? I have a friend with a cabin who has said he's not using it this weekend and we're free to use it."

"You do? We can? That sounds like a plan." She reached to kiss him. "Thank you for being just who you are."

Liem had grinned and kissed her back. He then turned them to walk out to the back porch and to the glider that Finnlea had brought from her home. It was becoming a favourite seat for them on the porch.

The sounds of night settled down around them as the moon and stars peeked out of the midnight sky. Little had Liem realized that when he had come to Finnlea's rescue all those weeks ago that he would have found the life of his life and the helpmeet that God had planned for him.

The couple was deeply in love, as new as it was, and planning for the short term of what they wanted to change about their home. It would come, they knew, as they amicably bickered over the changes, each willing to compromise for the other.

Night settled down even deeper as the two sat, reluctant to rise and head inside. They were content, despite what they had faced. God had been there for them and they could not turn away from Him.

Epilogue

A year later, Liem stood with his arms wrapped around Finnlea as he watched Lorcan and Eve mingling with their friends. Lorcan and Eve's wedding had just taken place. Liem could not be happier for his brother. Eve was just who Lorcan needed in his life.

Finnlea moved restlessly, a hand resting on her abdomen. Their little one was due soon and she felt uncomfortable. They were delighted to be expanding their family but today had been one of those rougher days that Finnlea had experienced.

Fergus and Sara stood nearby, glad for Lorcan and Eve. They had come to love this young couple as members of their family. Lora was near Lorcan and she was beaming with her happiness.

"Okay, sweetheart?" Liem kept his voice low, his concern for his bride evident in his tone.

"I am, love. Stop worrying. I am so happy for Lorcan and Eve."

"Me, too. Eve told me that you offered her part ownership in the store."

"I did. She deserves it. She has worked hard to build up the business. Lora wants to step away and I agree with that. I'll take over the online store. Eve will continue with the physical store. We're hiring. Eighteen months ago, I wasn't sure that I had made the right choice to open up a store here, especially with what we went through."

"I regret that we went through it. I just don't regret it as I met you." Liem dropped a kiss on her cheek. "I would have an empty life without you."

Finnlea leaned back against her groom. She still thought of him as that. God had blessed them in so many ways, she decided, even protecting them through it all. She felt called to walk closer and closer with Her Protector and she knew that Liem felt the same.

Moving away as the evening waned, Liem kept Finnlea's hand in his. He tucked her into her car and then stopped, a hand resting on the hood. He looked up, thanking God for His guidance and protection. Paul had sent a text message that Gibson had died of a heart attack while awaiting trial. That chapter of their lives were over. God was leading them off on a new one. All they had to do was follow Him.

Dear Readers

Thank you for picking up this adventure of Finnlea and Liem and being part of it. They went through an adventure that God allowed, only asking that they run to their Protector. And they did. Once more, the characters drove the story. And they didn't let the author in on why until near the end. This is typical of my characters.

God truly is our Protector. We try to walk our own way without His guidance. He calls us to come to Him. And our lives are fuller and richer when we do just that. We may move away from Him. He never moves and welcomes us back to our walk with Him when we do return. He never stops calling for us to do that.

Now, the characters who just had to walk in? Abe and Emma and their team tell their stories in the *His Guardians* series. Doug and Darcy are in *The Heart of a Lion*. Richard and his team are in the *His Protectors* series. My characters walk back and forth in books. I am always glad when Abe and Emma show up. They help to move the stories along.

This book was written as the April 2023 Camp Nanowrimo challenge. And it was quite the challenge this year. In March, I had shoulder surgery to repair a torn rotator cuff. Consequently on April 1, I began writing with only one hand. By the time I finished, I was back to using two hands even though I had to be very careful. God is providing healing for this.

As always, God bless each one of you in your daily walk with Him.

Ronna